# Decisions

# Decisions

## Consequences for Life, Society, and History

George A. Goens

ROWMAN & LITTLEFIELD
*Lanham • Boulder • New York • London*

Published by Rowman & Littlefield
An imprint of The Rowman & Littlefield Publishing Group, Inc.
4501 Forbes Boulevard, Suite 200, Lanham, Maryland 20706
www.rowman.com

86-90 Paul Street, London EC2A 4NE, United Kingdom

British Library Cataloguing in Publication Information Available

**Library of Congress Cataloging-in-Publication Data**
Names: Goens, George A., author.
Title: Decisions : consequences for life, society, and history / George A. Goens.
Description: Lanham : Rowman & Littlefield, [2022] | Includes bibliographical
    references and index. | Summary: "This book discusses the challenges educators face
    in understanding communication and decisions and their effects on the economy,
    society, democracy, and the meaning of life"—Provided by publisher.
Identifiers: LCCN 2022027637 (print) | LCCN 2022027638 (ebook) | ISBN
    9781475863673 (cloth) | ISBN 9781475863680 (paperback) | ISBN
    9781475863697 (epub)
Subjects: LCSH: Decision making.
Classification: LCC BF448 .G66 2022  (print) | LCC BF448  (ebook) | DDC
    153.8/3—dc23/eng/20220812
LC record available at https://lccn.loc.gov/2022027637
LC ebook record available at https://lccn.loc.gov/2022027638

*For family and friends—present and past*

# Contents

# Preface

Decisions direct one's life. Living requires choices—many of them. In that sense, everyone is alike, although our lives do not follow the same path or reach the same outcome. Some decisions are of little magnitude, and others are of great significance and consequence. Sometimes we don't even know the magnitude of decisions when we are making them. But at other times, decisions are exacting, heartrending, lifesaving, or final.

Most people do not realize the number of decisions they make each day. Some sources indicate that adults make about thirty-five thousand decisions in a day. Individuals make 226 decisions per day concerning food alone, according to a study by Cornell University.[1] It sounds unreasonable that individuals make that number of decisions daily.

Many decisions are mundane—for example, deciding what to wear or what to eat for breakfast. These are choices of minor magnitude. However, even daily and usually routine decisions may be consequential. Small choices can have major outcomes, leading to unforeseen events, unexpected reactions from others, or unanticipated results. And even the choice not to decide is a decision.

Beyond the personal realm, some roles, especially leadership roles, require decision-making that affects the operation or the results of an organization and the lives of others. In this context, too, decisions may be minor and relatively innocuous, or they may seem routine but have huge repercussions. As responsibilities or events escalate, decisions can have a larger and deeper influence. They not only relate to knowledge and professional and social contexts but also concern the values of formal and informal relationships and their effects on individuals and organizations.

Organizations, like life itself, exist in an uncertain and at times chaotic context. Seemingly minor issues or events can have a dramatic impact because organizations and society do not always work in a clear-cut, linear manner. Small occurrences or events can have large, nonlinear impacts on society, organizations, or relationships. Almost everyone can recall times when a seemingly minor decision altered the larger picture with surprising impact.

This also happens personally. For example, Luke decides not to go golfing and instead goes to his friend's house and meets a woman, goes on a date with her, and eventually marries her. If he had gone to hit golf balls, he would not have met her, they would not have dated, and a birdie on the sixth hole would have been his only achievement, not a lifelong relationship.

Decisions create the life people live. We are all active participants, not always passive bystanders. Decision-making occurs not only on the relatively small scale of an individual's life, but also in the larger frame of society, organizations, and politics. Individuals and their solitary or collective decisions create the world in which we live both individually and collectively.

Decisions—reactionary to others or independent—take place every day in a variety of circumstances and conditions. Recognizing the intent and content of these decisions is important for life. Decisions should be based on developing caring and loving relationships with others built around love, kindness, and service.

## NOTE

1. Frank Graff, "How Many Daily Decisions Do We Make?" *UNC-TV Science*, February 7, 2018, http://science.unctv.org/content/reportersblog/choices.

# Chapter 1

# Decisions

Life is the sum of all your choices.

—Albert Camus

The reason I talk to myself is because I'm the only one whose answers I accept.

—George Carlin

Life is not always easy, and goodness does not always prevail. Life goes in a multitude of directions. Writing a poem brings understanding and satisfaction. Frustration mounts as ideals are compromised. Death happens and sadness overwhelms. Tackling an ethical issue and speaking out brings a sense of duty and justice.

Two basic questions follow people throughout their lives. The first is "Who am I?"—that is, what values and principles define us? In many cases, our search for an answer raises the second question: "Why am I here?" Actually, the answer to that question has far more to do with meaning than happiness or pain avoidance. Self-understanding does not come from simply taking a course or watching a video or reading a self-help book. It doesn't happen overnight. And it is far more than simply selecting a career or an occupation.

Popular movies, in their formulaic way, gloss over the difficulty and complexity of confronting life and finding understanding and insight. In most films, a character faces a situation, applies him- or herself, confronts a setback, and eventually succeeds in finding a heartwarming solution. In real life, however, lightning doesn't strike, heroes do not ride over the hill, and success and happiness don't always spring to life in ninety minutes.

Meaning in life can be circumvented by ego and connection to self-esteem and self-importance. It is not about a primary focus on oneself or reaching a level of importance, popularity, or recognition. Meaning does not come from egotistical or self-oriented commitments or perspectives.

Viktor Frankl's iconic book *Man's Search for Meaning* provides an intense discussion of life and meaning, emanating from his time as a concentration camp inmate during the Holocaust. He was a neurologist and psychiatrist who became known for logotherapy and existential analysis, which are considered the third Viennese school of psychotherapy.

Frankl's experiences in the concentration camp shaped his understanding of reality and the meaning of human life. During this time, he found that those people who did not lose a sense of purpose and meaning in life survived much longer than others who lost their way.[1] Frankl believed that life has meaning under all circumstances, both positive and negative.

The main motivation in life is to find meaning, which doesn't come from materialism, narcissism, or fame. Meaninglessness darkens perspective and destroys the imperative to decide and act.

Frankl stated that individuals cannot control what happens to them in life. However, everyone is in singular control and has total freedom over one thing: how they respond to life's situations and circumstances. Only the individual can determine how they are going to respond; our response can be a singular, personal, and empowering decision. External forces may take away a person's control over many things, but not their control over their individual reactions.

Facing an unexpected death—for example, for children who lost a parent—is excruciating and unbelievable, especially at an early age. When she was four years old, Claire Bower's mother died of complications while giving birth to Claire's brother. In a speech she gave in 2016 for Every Mother Counts, a nonprofit organization founded by Christy Turlington and dedicated to making childbirth safer, Claire wrote:

> Growing up was hard, there is no possible way to sugar coat that; I would be lying if I said it was easy.
>
> When I was growing up, I would often try to suppress my own emotions simply so that I would feel strong and like I had accomplished something, when truly, ignoring the reality of my emotions and failing to face them head on accomplished absolutely nothing but prolonged heartache. Learning to face the emotions, the heartache, and the loss was a day-to-day learning process but one that to this day has made me who I am.
>
> Moreover, it taught me that through hardships we must find courage, confront our own emotions, grow wiser through experience, and learn to cope with the situation so that we do not live the rest of our lives dwelling within a shadow of loss. These lessons have made me strong and have given me a much different perspective of the concept of life, along with its purpose.

Growing up without my biological mother was not easy, but it did teach me something. I cannot change what has happened to me, but I can take the negative things that have happened in the past 16 years, and I can consciously choose to use them to make a positive impact and find a purpose. If using my story and what I have learned from my experience to spread awareness can help one person, it has helped somebody and I have served a purpose. That is what is now important to me.

At the end of your life will you be proud of what you did and who you impacted? That is what we should all be asking ourselves. So let's all step out, find our purpose, and fulfill it.[2]

Claire's speech, given when she was a sixteen-year-old, demonstrates a wise maturity and fortitude. Rising up and not adopting a victim mentality illustrates Frankl's point. People, even young ones, can decide how they are going to react to situations, even heartbreaking ones.

Finding significance in life—the central core of the question "Why am I here?"—is a primary, not a secondary, motivation. This basically requires, not passive deference to others, but striving and struggling for a worthwhile goal.

Frankl stated, "Ultimately, a man should not ask what the meaning of his life is, but rather he must recognize that it is he who is asked. In a word, each man is questioned by life; and he can only answer to life by answering for his own life; to life he can only respond by being responsible."[3] Frankl thought that meaning is possible in spite of suffering because in life, at times, suffering is unavoidable. He cites three ways to discover meaning.

One way is by creating work or doing a deed: helping others, acting honorably, ensuring ethics are a consideration in decisions, and working to enhance the dignity and respect of others—children, aged, poor, troubled, or suffering.

The second way is to find meaning through experiencing nature or the great ideas of goodness, truth, and beauty. Principles and ideas open the heart and mind to understanding and meaning.

Finally, suffering also brings meaning because when individuals are confronted, for example, with an illness, they are challenged to change themselves. Sometimes the sacrifice one must make in these circumstances brings greater meaning to life.

Frankl suggests, "Live as if you are living already for the second time and as if you had acted the first time as wrongly as you are about to act now!" It is true what he says: "Each man is questioned by life; and he can only answer to life by answering for his own life; to life he can only respond by being responsible."[4]

## FINAL WORDS: MEANING, PURPOSE, AND HAPPINESS

Individuals want to extend themselves and move beyond a manufactured life based on ego needs and seeking the golden ring of success. Instead of simply trying to be happy and living a life others expect, individuals must become attached to something greater than themselves. People want to apply their strengths to something meaningful, not just to the trivial or lucrative.

Fred Kofman identifies four pillars that intrinsically motivate people in pursuing something greater:

- Purpose: significance, meaning, impact, service, and self-transcendence
- Principles: integrity, ethics, morality, goodness, truth, and dignity
- People: belonging, connection, community, recognition, respect, and praise
- Freedom: creativity, achievement, learning, and self-mastery[5]

In answering the question "Why am I here?" everyone must look inward and determine the values on which they stand, what behavior makes them true to themselves, and what approach will be honorable to their efforts, regardless of whether they are successful or not.

Love, wisdom, courage, justice, and temperance are qualities of character that build relationships with others and establish a framework for determining what is meaningful and how to address conditions and circumstances. Meaningful actions are right, justifiable, and good. Narcissistic deceit and cheating may win at times, but they do not create meaning and ultimately diminish character and self-worth.

Life is not simple. It comes with unknowns, questions, events, and issues that, in many cases, do not always have straightforward or clear answers or directions. Everyone is born in unique circumstances because families differ, geography is not the same, and there are distinct philosophies and values of family and society. Humans face an open book of decisions they must make in a world filled with natural laws of science as well as chaos, emotion, expectations, and the unknown.

Life requires decisions in all of its stages. Even as toddlers and in childhood and their teen years, boys and girls learn to make decisions. As adults, the decisions become more complex and difficult as individuals confront personal, family, educational, and professional concerns that are not always discreet or judicious. Things frequently become interwoven and complicated, affecting the knowns and unknowns of life.

Life presents some decisions that are almost predetermined just by following the expected pattern, course, or ritual. Do what is right by meeting predetermined standards. People accomplish what is expected in an established and principled way. In some professions, making decisions—what and how—must follow processes and procedures. In other situations, circumstances are not predetermined or familiar to individuals or communities. Artificial intelligence (AI) is a prime example. As AI develops, it presents major opportunities and issues across most aspects of society.

Many perceived discussions are strictly a cognitive experience from which choices are made from various options. In some cases, they can be anticipated and even habitual. But life is not strictly following a script. Cognitive, rational, and scientific analysis can bring unexpected conditional and innovative approaches.

Individuals, however, are not computers operating under rationally defined algorithms and written to complete tasks or make decisions. Following calculated steps is not always the answer. Problem-solving can be complex and is not open to calculating or computer-based solutions. People are not programmed, and life is not simply a list of routine activities.

Life is replete with unstructured and random concerns, often creating complex and sometimes ill-defined questions and issues that are not always in the direct control of individuals. The unforeseen and unexpected occur sometimes, requiring fortitude and reasoning to address them. Issues and pathways are not always clear.

Life does not unfold in a linear manner. Things are not always predictable or sequential. Some individuals believe in the myth that decision-making is always a linear activity—simply follow the suggested sequence from start to finish and a good decision will formulate. In fact, there may be stops and starts, going back, then jumping ahead, based on the unfolding situation, characters, and time. Circumstances dictate the flow and process of decisions. Sometimes conditions change, unknowns become clear, and timing unfolds more quickly or alters.

Organizations engage in a number of different types of plans. Some involve operations—processes and procedures—and some are for planning—strategic and otherwise—involving the long-range picture, vision, and mission, all of which require a perspective on the entire organization and a focus on long-term expectations and outcomes.

In addition, strategic and operational plans are technical and include contingency proposals. Tactical planning supports strategic planning because it involves the plans, strategies, processes, and actions necessary to achieve it. Basically, its focus is on what needs to happen and when to achieve the strategic goals.

In all types of organized planning, strategies and events happen according to expectations and thinking. Unforeseen obstacles and events occur, altering the larger picture, systems, or events and at times requiring changes. Nothing works like a clock, except a clock, and even then problems can arise. People come with expectations and varied perceptions and philosophies. Efficiency is another myth of perfect planning and decision-making. As desirable as efficiency is, it is not always affective and succumbs to human and life circumstances.

Some individuals, as the old adage states, should "look before they leap," yet they move to make quick decisions. What gets in the way is that individuals want to demonstrate their knowledge and authority, and others make quick decisions because of a lack of clarity on circumstances and the presence of uncertain factors.

In addition is the image of a decisive leader, but being decisive can be wrong. At times, rushing ahead comes with ignoring or avoiding making a decision because of the time it takes. Putting off making a decision to gather more research or data may pay big dividends. When an emergency does not exist, delaying a decision may be beneficial because it may help focus attention on an issue of higher priority.

The circumstances and impact of decisions may require greater input than simply that of the person in charge and with the responsibility for making them. The context of the decision and its ramifications may require knowledge and viewpoints from others. Partial resolution of issues or questions may require more time or instigate deeper issues or complications. Leaders have to understand decisions are not without implications or other issues. In addition, others may have to be involved because accuracy and content must be as precise as possible.

Some leaders have an arrogant perspective and perceive themselves to be "right" and want only data or opinions that support their position. Any contrary data or information is not desired or tolerated. Such leaders refrain from examining limitations or inaccuracies of their position. They become blind to circumstances and potential concerns or other options present. People who simply make decisions that they prefer without examining other information or options close themselves off from the possibility of making better decisions. Some of these leaders think there is only one way to address the issue and that they have the perspective and experience to resolve it.

The myth associated with this approach to decisions is false.[6] Time is required in decision-making, and rational individuals have to make good decisions about high-stakes issues on their own. One person's rational conclusion may not be rational to others and to the context. All situations are not predictable or clearly defined.

## DECISIONS AND IMPACT

Decisions and their impact reveal the road traveled in life. The same is true for organizations and governments—decisions create the pavement and direction into the future, and what is down the road is not always evident.

What people confront are not simply issues of their own making. They live in a society, community, state, and nation. What an individual or community determines has repercussions for the bigger picture and vice versa.

State- or national-level government issues generate concerns and matters at the personal or local level that need to be addressed. Decisions at the top trickle down, requiring each person or organization to make choices to support, debate, or commit to actions through fiscal or personal involvement.

Historical decisions importantly change the nature of governance and prospects for the future. Signing the Declaration of Independence altered the character and government of the United States. The South seceding from the union and the resulting Civil War altered state regulations and universal rights for all citizens.

The Louisiana Purchase and passing the Civil Rights Act expanded the country and had a major influence on the scope and power of the United States. In addition, the use of the atomic bomb to end World War II played a major role in the world's interactions and agenda. History's scope was greatly enlarged by the moon landing and subsequent actions in outer space and with the planets. All of these decisions and actions elevated ambitions and concerns, as most transformative events or activities do.

Today, the world is transforming because the economy is moving from physical labor to knowledge-based production, artificial intelligence, research, and application. Knowledge, value, and innovation are essential today in addressing a transformational future.

Decisions define a country's and a person's values and the nature of their philosophy and personality. Character defines decisions by their focus and consequences. Decisions are made in very complex circumstances to achieve better outcomes, which is not always easy to do. Rationality does not always work in a nonrational context, where feelings, desires, and personal interests and unknowns are present.

Risk is always a factor in any context. Certainly, national decisions, as well as large, corporate decisions, have complex layers and circumstances. Risks are not always observable or discernible. Uncertainty comes because the probability of an outcome is unknowable.[7] Landing on the moon was not without risk humanly, politically, and economically.

Over time, decisions evolve from individuals making judgments principally by themselves to group dynamics and participatory rulings. Groups, however, can be susceptible to "groupthink," which pushes for unanimity and can often stop investigation and research of alternative perspectives, thoughts, and actions.

Frequently, people indicate they use their intuition and feelings to make the decision to buy a house, determine a course of action, or get off the mark. Instinct, along with intuition, is used to move ahead. The courage to make these kinds of decisions is admirable. Frequently, a "gut-based" response is used in times of crisis—instinct is applied to intuitive decisions.

## CONTEXT

Conflict exists in how people perceive the world. Scientific thinking at times conflicts with reality and its seemingly chaotic manner. Events and relationships do not always follow the course of the scientific method. The question is, do science and the scientific method without doubt explain life and the behavior of people?

Cognitive reasoning and emotion are both used when examining lives and making decisions. Reasoning and emotions are not always congruent; one can supersede the other, depending on the circumstance and its rationality or emotional passion and fervor.

Reason is based on the line of thought and rationality. Deduction and logic are involved in reasoning; objectivity is based on facts and unbiased research. Emotion, however, moves from a strictly cognitive act to one concerning feelings and passions that are experienced consciously—fear, joy, sorrow, love. Emotional reactions are not always predictable or related to logic or science. Passion carries a heartfelt drive that can happen spontaneously.

Decisions are not always linear, following a sequence of steps. In fact, some decisions require circling back to the first step of why a decision has to be made or reviewing the criteria for a successful outcome. Some decisions rest on the measurable, and others on sentiment. When one falls in love, is it based on metrics?

Some decisions are programmed in how they are made.[8] Organizational and operational decisions usually stipulate process and evidence. Research, if it is to be accepted, must be based on correctly conducted processes and have specific decision-making criteria and validity. And finally, choices concerning opportunities are significant. Some people perceive decisions to open doors to opportunity or resolve issues. Subjective judgments at times define possible opportunities that others do not see.

In life, there are decisions with no clear means of approach. Intuition may play a large part, along with personal preferences and values and past experiences and beliefs. Subjective judgments are a part of these decisions when a specific process or regulation is not present. Uncertainty, however, is always a factor, whether in objective or subjective decisions.

Personal decisions are just that—unstructured, subjective, uncertain, and beyond routine or systems. They affect individuals and can consist of objective and subjective content and issues. Personal interests are intrinsic because of experience, expectations, values, and a host of other influences. Personal biases or emotions are often involved in defining and determining perspectives and options.

Strategic decisions are based on the nature of personal decisions. How one reacts to these individualized circumstances is based on a large number of opinions and conclusions derived from each life story. Intuition is a major factor, as are one's values and principled commitments. Sometimes strategies are clearly apparent, but at other times there is no clear action or decision to address the concerns.

Opportunity comes and goes depending on a variety of factors. Foresight can be a factor, and commitment to certain issues can drive people to act. Loyalty to causes or individuals energizes people to become aware and involved. Strategic decisions arise that can lead to progress on individual or collective goals.

## IMPORTANT ISSUES IN DECISION-MAKING

The mind and perception are essential aspects of confronting situations and circumstances and addressing them. Some conditions require specific knowledge and data in order to consider them. Reliably, expertise is necessary to perceive the major and subtle concerns around issues and outcomes. This often leads to determining the nature of the decision-making process.

An obvious style taught in college courses is rational: a sequential model that examines the specific circumstances and causes, identifies possible decision options, and determines the best solution alternative based on the logical and measurable pros and cons. Structure and reason are at the core of a rational decision-making process.

Another decision-making option is intuition, which does not rest on the scientific scale of the decision-making ledger. A decision "feels" right as an individual concentrates on the issue and concludes that a response fits the situation and feels appropriate cognitively and emotionally. Such decisions are not without brain power; they are choices made based on a sense of rationality and emotional assessment.

In many of these situations, all of the information may not be available, which requires some understanding of the field or content involved. Individuals cannot make an intuitive decision in fields they have little

information about or where they have no understanding of the general consequences ethically, conceptually, or legally. These would simply be guesses.
Guessing is speculation that may be devoid of facts or insight.

Decision-making should be dependent on social truths, values, and contemporary research and knowledge. Facts and data are necessary. However,
procrastination and avoidance can result from an individual's lack of confidence or dependency on others. Dependency on others and their approval is a
deterrent to speaking out and a road to a darkened sense of self.

On the other hand, there are individuals who want to "direct traffic." They
exude confidence but do not always know or understand their limitations.
They may not have the required knowledge or experience to lead and make
judgments. Sometimes unearned self-esteem is at play, creating distraction
and group turmoil.

Some individuals only consider evidence and data that confirm their perspective and opinion. They do not want to examine all sides of the issue or
options for moving forward, even though understanding alternatives about the
matter or problem is paramount in defining significant issues and direction.

## PSYCHOLOGICAL ISSUES

All decisions have consequences. Minor ones are made every day from the
time of awakening until bedtime. Other decisions are highly consequential and involve not only facts and goals but also the psychology behind
decision-making.[9]

Most of the decisions people make are done unconsciously. Information
processing occurs subconsciously, but this does not mean such decisions are
irrational. It simply means that the thought process can be both a conscious
motivation and also an unconscious intuition.

Unconscious or intuitive decisions are faster than conscious deliberations.
Most individuals act "instinctively and quickly" in crisis circumstances.
People's minds work extremely fast. Individuals learn intuitive behavior in
crisis or emergency conditions. In a sense, the unconscious mind protects individuals from danger by taking control and overwriting the conscious mind.

At times, individuals feel exasperated at limitations and desire more choices
and information. While individuals may feel this way, "the more options we
have, the harder our decision-making will be."[10] Sometimes individuals think
and review situations and then get frustrated with a number of options.

People think decision-making comes with control. The opportunity to
choose feels like control. Individuals want their decisions to have an effect.
This is important. Inconsequential decisions or involvement can be time

wasting and cause individuals to lose faith in the process. They want to have some positive effect.

Decision-making is not strictly a cognitive process. Moods and attitudes can have an effect on whether they are made rationally or more intuitively. People are different. Some are more likely to rely on intuition, while others prefer following a predictable "rational" process. The style of decision-making also depends on the circumstances and what is at stake.

A general inclination exists that groups make better decisions because of the variety of perspectives and experiences. Individuals make personal decisions often in solitude, without external opinions. Should a group decide whether or not one should get married? Should a group determine annual organizational goals?

While there are advantages to a group decision, there is the problem of groupthink, which causes individuals to stifle their opinions or emotions and go with the group, particularly if they are in conflict with the group or its history. The way things were traditionally done carries great weight. Disrupting conformity and connections often causes silence in order to maintain harmony. Taking a stance against convention is not easy but important at times. Too often, when people are in doubt, they allow others to decide.

## CONTROL

Individuals often state that they do not control anything, that their life is the domain of others. They interpret control as simply choices, power, and authority. That is a mistake in perspective.

Everyone has total power over how they respond to situations and the decisions of others. This power exists in personal and professional life. In addition, citizens have the power of the ballot and participation in the political system and activities. Adults and parents control expenditures, relationships, time, resources, and the means of expression.

In a sense, everyone has a story to tell through their lives. Doing so requires integrity in one's life and values. What story does one want to tell—the principles, values, talents, beliefs? Life stories do not need a Hollywood writer, physical action, and triumph. Dirty Harry lives in movies, not down the block.

People often think too little of their own lives. The media highlights the politicians, the wealthy, entertainers, and others. The term *rock star* is emblematic of today's culture. People generally do not consider the neighborhood mechanic, the English teacher, Dorothy the nurse, Jim the postal worker, the waitress or bartender, or the local police officer to be heroes or heroic. But each of them is indispensable in some way to somebody and to society. The impact of neighbors, coworkers, children, spouses, and others may not be known to the general public, but to individuals they may be critical for life, personal philosophy, and success.

The stories of people's lives are much deeper. The uncle who helps his nephew whose father died when the boy was four years old. The history teacher who tells a student that the paper he has written is one of the best in all his years of classes. The neighbor who says to the kids, "Quit fighting. You know, someday you'll need each other. Show some love and care. That's what they taught me in the army in Vietnam."

Children can learn wisdom from their parents, relatives, teachers, neighbors, and others. No one is too young or too old for those lessons. Ask a relative or a successful person, and they will indicate the impact of other individuals on them and their success.


## DO THEY EVER STOP?

Is there any time in life when decisions are not prevalent? People sometimes think that the number and importance of decisions dwindle as we grow older. Looking back on careers, professions, family, or community, some feel their lives are less important and vibrant than they used to be. What is too often forgotten is the influence of individuals on others. Age does not matter when it comes to influence and impact.

Listen to people who explain the course of their lives and the people or events that were transformational. Generally, it is a person who helped them understand circumstances, their talents, or most importantly their confidence that provided the foundation for moving ahead. These others frequently see more depth and ability in us than we see in ourselves.

Almost everyone perceives decisions as totally rational: metrics, analysis, fiscal estimates of success. Many people feel that metrics accurately provide a means to determine intangibles like attitude, creativity, and intellectual ability or consistency of results.

But skews or biases can be buried in metrical measurements, depending on how data is measured, the nature of the data and questions, and how the results are gathered and appraised and by whom.

Any metrical approach to data collection must be precise and accurate; otherwise, the data will be useless. Accuracy is important in order to discern whether projections and results are valid and true. Data in investigating outcomes and issues is valid only if defined, composed, and collected properly.

Conclusions can only be drawn if the data and information are relevant and properly collected. Formal judgments can only be made through resolving questions—determining that an issue exists and gathering data and information are necessary to complete a diagnosis, judgment, and conclusion.

All individuals need the proficiency to choose between options and alternatives, one of which is to decide whether or not to make a decision. Sometimes staying in place is the correct call—do nothing. In other cases, determinations must be made about desired outcomes, timing, involvement of others, and pros and cons of potential results. Also important is the responsibility for implementing the decision.

Determining what proficiencies are important in making and implementing decisions is critical because decision-making involves content, intent, and consequence. Decisions are more complicated than people may think because they have impacts on relationships, finances, roles, emotions, and other vital aspects of life. Even routine decisions can have major and larger impacts.

Decisions also relate to the strategies used to make them. They depend on the nature of the issue and its timing, and the nature of relationships, both formal and informal, as well as professional. Sometimes, in retrospect, an individual's assessment of the issue will question not only the content of the decision but also how it was made. Not everyone uses the same process or manner to determine how decisions are made because they depend on the issue, emotion, and intention, which should drive the process.

People who want to appear decisive can be impulsive, which may not be the best approach because the first impulse is not always correct. Certainly, the issue at stake is critical in determining the approach necessary to make a correct and impactful decision.

Several other styles can be problematic.[11] Or approaches to decisions could include compliance—basically, selecting the most pleasing, popular, or comfortable option. Other issues may require delegating to others, who are then trusted to make such a decision. Other approaches to decision-making try to balance and weigh the factors of the decision and then use the information to make a well-informed decision. Studying and analyzing the options and information allows for properly appraising the possible outcomes at stake.

Finally, another strategy is to reflect on and prioritize the options, especially for decisions that have the largest and greatest impact. Issues of importance affecting others require effort and energy to determine the best option and approach.

In this approach, rationality is considered, but intuitive knowledge may also be at play. All different approaches are applied, depending on the issue, in personal, professional, or organizational matters.

## NOTES

1. Viktor Frankl, *Man's Search for Meaning* (New York: Washington Square Press, 1984).

2. Claire A. Bower, "From a Child's Eyes: Loss, Growth and Purpose," *Every Mother Counts* (blog), April 1, 2016, https://blog.everymothercounts.org/from-a -childs-eyes-loss-growth-and-purpose-dc986e157c72.

3. Frankl, *Man's Search for Meaning*, 109.

4. Frankl, *Man's Search for Meaning*, 109.

5. Fred Kofman, *The Meaning Revolution: Leading with the Power of Purpose* (New York: Currency, 2018), 121–27.

6. Cheryl Strauss Einhorn, "11 Myths about Decision-Making," *Harvard Business Review*, April 20, 2021, https://hbr.org/2021/04/11-myths-about-decision-making.

7. Leigh Buchanan and Andrew O'Connell, "A Brief History of Decision Making," *Harvard Business Review*, January 2006, https://hbr.org/2006/01/a-brief-history-of -decision-making.

8. "Types of Decisions: Programmed and Non-Programmed," Business Manage-ment Ideas, https://www.businessmanagementideas.com/decision-making/types-of -decisions-programmed-and-non-programmed/4831.

9. Alex Devero, "Psychology of Design Masterclass—7 Important Facts about Decision Making," blog, July 4, 2016, https://blog.alexdevero.com/psychology -design-pt9-decision-making/.

10. Devero, "Psychology of Design Masterclass."

11. Frank Graff, "How Many Daily Decisions Do We Make?," UNCTV.org, Febru-ary 7, 2018.

*Chapter 2*

# Life's Path

You must be willing to leave the life you planned in order to find the one waiting for you.

—Joseph Campbell

If you chase two rabbits, both will escape.

—Unknown

Life is a fluid puzzle. Every person in our lives is a piece of that puzzle with their unique footprint. Each is different in shape and size, yet collectively they all fit together, interconnecting and binding to create a distinctive image. Each person is significant in their idiosyncratic way of making their life's picture whole.

At times, a piece is lost and a vacancy exists, crying out for connection and wholeness. Inevitably, whole pieces are lost forever—destiny and personal choices are at play. Fate intervenes or people decide to exit. The picture must reform and construct new links and associations.

While the new picture maintains some resemblance to the old, it is different—relationships alter, some bind together more strongly, and others become more distant. The picture takes on a different look and point of view. It evolves, sometimes slowly and sometimes unexpectedly and quickly. Some pieces disassemble into solitary ones, still uniquely shaped but alone, detached from the entire image. The pattern rearranges, and each remaining piece reshapes and reconnects. Sometimes the individual piece reformulates itself through self-reflection, the proximity and influence of others, or the wear and tear of events.

The change is dramatic or subtle, but powerful, when a piece is suddenly out of the picture. One change causes relationships to reshape, transform, or end as individuals adjust to the loss of their loved one's personality, values, and perspective. Individuals still remember the piece that was lost and what it brought to the total picture of life.

Children search for who they are—to find and know themselves. They seek their identity, how they connect, and where they fit. Do they want to be the main focus, sit quietly in the background, or be the distinctive piece that provides emotional and structural meaning?

Children create pictures of what their lives are going to be as dreams and aspirations take form in their minds. That may work out for some, but for many others—the vast majority—the puzzle of life has little relationship to the picture they had in their mind as a child. Some do not realize that other pieces affect and influence their position and connections—intangibles direct connections and experiences.

Life does not evolve by simply and logically putting puzzle pieces together or creating an engineered flowchart. Logic and reason do not always control direction and impact. Emotions exist. Spontaneity shapes decisions. Other people intervene. Serendipitous events and meetings refigure lives, and unexpected losses and deaths alter relationships and perspectives.

The puzzle of life creates different contours and dimensions. While it may have the same elements, it still transforms. Wear and tear affect connections. Colors evolve, sometimes brighter, other times darker, with shifting boldness and subtlety. Energy shifts and perspective changes. Some of these adjustments emerge slowly, and others explosively and quickly. Experience alters and lightens the interpretation and impact.

Of course, new pieces are added. Births transform the picture with their distinctive impact and hopes. New loving relationships do the same thing, in many cases, polishing rough edges and modifying outlooks and connections. They also alter the puzzle's viewpoint, as pieces from the past become a smaller part of the frame, while others grow in size and consequence.

Life can seem confusing, like one thousand pieces of an abstract puzzle without a clear final picture. Life configures itself mysteriously and dramatically at times. The wonder of it all is life's beauty and unpredictability; otherwise, it would be trite and boring if cast in stone. Life emerges and is coupled together by personal decisions, passions, emotions, and relationships, hopefully predicated on clear and honorable values and principles, which can be the glue that keeps the pieces together.

Children look at the world with wonder. Flowers and birds with their unique shapes and colors capture their attention. The variety of noises and movements cause them to stop, look, and listen. The mysteries of nature stimulate curiosity. Kindergartners wonder about how things happen and work.

Erik Erikson's theory of psychosocial development explains human development psychologically and the tensions individuals feel.[1] Success is achieved through a healthy personality. Failure, however, can instill a sense of inadequacy, leading to difficulty in working through the challenges of life.

Erikson's eight psychological stages are defined in table 2.1, along with the tensions in each stage. Human development moves beyond physical development and has a maturation pattern. Everyone does not experience the stages in lockstep or for the same length of time. Growth is a process over time and a means for dialogue, self-discovery, and understanding.

In adulthood, communication expands beyond simple personal family dialogue. As responsibilities increase, so do the realm and impact of decisions. Personal decisions are largely focused on self, family members, personal finances, relationships, political issues, and others. Adult life expands beyond the small circle of friends to community, organizations, and larger geographic associations in society.

Tensions come to life. Hopefully, individuals do not stagnate but develop the ability to reflect wisely about self, community, and life itself. Ethics and ethical challenges require analysis, choice, and action. Insight should lead to responsible action, and issues of principle must be addressed. Principles should and must guide behavior and decisions because they are the foundation for behaving ethically, which leads to responsible action. Principles require people to act, not just verbalize and discuss them. Many parents will say to a child, "What were you thinking?" Sometimes children do act without any thought of the correctness, ethics, or appropriateness of decisions.

Philosophy is not just an abstract statement about living life with principles and ethics. It must be applied to all decisions, and there are no easy answers. Interpreting events and determining what is ethical and proper is not simple. Individuals must be able to examine circumstances and define the ethical conditions at stake, the nature of the options available based on those ethics, and the means and methods to implement them.

Sometimes determining ethics and consequences is not without trauma. Decisions may include loss of life. Harry Truman's decision to drop an atomic

**Table 2.1. Erikson's Eight Psychological Stages**

| Stage | Tensions | | |
|---|---|---|---|
| Infancy | Basic trust | vs. | Mistrust |
| Early childhood | Autonomy | vs. | Shame and doubt |
| Preschool, age 3–5 | Initiative | vs. | Guilt |
| Age 5–12 | Industry | vs. | Inferiority |
| Teenage years | Identity | vs. | Role confusion |
| Young adulthood | Intimacy | vs. | Isolation |
| Age 40–65 | Generativity | vs. | Stagnation |
| Age 65–death | Reflection | to | Wisdom |

Source: Erik Erikson, Psychological Stages. https://www.ncbi.nlm.nih.gov/books/NBK556096

bomb on two Japanese cities filled with citizens and children was made to save lives by ending the war, thus avoiding a larger death toll. Reporters indicated that a normative type of invasion and landing in Japan would have cost an estimated million casualties. Some individuals perceived no difference between firebombing Dresden and the atomic bombing of Hiroshima.[2]

Thinking and mindsets determine the course and direction of decisions. Sometimes people have no clue about what they think and their evaluation of situations and circumstances. Even individuals with biased views, partial information, and speculative data move forward and make decisions. Often individuals simply make decisions on the basis of the past, the opinions of friends or others, or to maintain the impressions others have of them.

Listening, thinking, and understanding are not easy. Time often pushes decisions. In some issues and emergencies, timely and quick decisions must be made, such as by emergency responders, police officers, and firefighters. Too often, however, individuals do not want to take the appropriate time to make a decision, and ignorance or peer pressure may be at play.

Decision-making is done a number of ways. For example, scientists, physicians, and other professionals apply the scientific method. Others must be able to apply intuition in actively unfolding circumstances such as police calls. In all decision-making situations, known and unknown risks are at play. In most cases, individuals must "make the case" for adoption and action.

Moral decisions are difficult, and people frequently rely on their intuition when facing difficult moral decisions and outcomes. In these cases, individuals' ethical instruments are a powerful influence. People are not machines driven by an algorithm. When facing decisions, they see the world through intellect as well as emotion and experience.

Individuals must explain and justify their decisions—in some cases, why they made a decision to move forward or why they refused to follow a particular mandate or expectation. The issue may involve moral questions, as well as leadership or organizational values and expectations. Leaders have a responsibility for explaining decisions.

In right-versus-right decisions, there may be two or more "right" ways to address a problem. Life carries many complicated issues for making determinations. The right course of action is not easy and carries different residual implications and impacts. Leaders' decisions reveal and test their values.[3]

## HISTORY OF DECISION-MAKING

The success or failure of a presidency is determined by the depth and quality of decisions made. Those judgments are reflected in the course the country took and the evident outcomes. There is always risk, some potentially affecting the quality of life or even life itself. Sometimes quality decisions fail because of the means or methods used to implement them. Good decisions do not always produce effective or desired results. The outcomes of decisions determine whether they were successful.

Truman got the result he wanted by applying a nuclear weapon. Some argue the outcome was the end of the war, but the manner in which it was achieved threatened civilization in the future. To this day, atomic and nuclear weaponry remain a major concern in international and other affairs.

Life moves at different tempos, which influences the complexity of situations. In some circumstances, it is difficult even to determine the exact nature of the issue, its depth, and corollary questions. Not everyone has the background knowledge and skill to determine accurately the essence of the matter, questions, and potential repercussions. Hence, the possible solutions can be limited and erroneous. Reciprocal issues can explode the state of affairs. Individuals can be excessively optimistic or terribly erroneous in framing choices.

Risk is a part of all decisions. Most of the time, it is relatively minor, but sometimes it is considerable. In marriages and other relationships, personal responses or actions can create major problems and concerns. In emotional times, comments or expressions can subvert the trust and understanding between people.

Organizations and corporations, like individuals, must confront risk. They have to plan for the future and for success, but they also have to plan for the worst. Many people only look at the "bright side" because they don't want to be negative. In life, sometimes there are limited opportunities to achieve what one desires. Not taking a shot will remain for the rest of one's life. "I wonder what would have happened if . . . ?" is a question that arises in quiet moments or in daydreams, particularly as one ages and reflects back on life.

Uncertainty raises risk. Whether or not you've identified variables, forces, or history can increase the odds of failure or be the cause of success. In both cases, there are hazards. If unknown causes and issues are key factors in success, then one's choice can be based on an erroneous analysis. False interpretation of a perceived decision can create conflict or failure because it is based on a incorrect interpretation and examination.

Social, political, and economic systems operate in a chaotic context. Small issues or forces can produce huge events—as meteorologist Edward Lorenz stated, a famous "butterfly effect."[4] The flapping of a butterfly's wings in China can cause a tornado in Nebraska. The butterfly effect is also present in organizations, social circles, and relationships. A husband's or wife's comment can produce a rupture in communication. In larger organizations, the same is true. Individuals—bosses or workers—can misread the tenor of the organization, people, expectations, principles, and values.

Logic does not always rule. People's priorities and expectations do not always connect. What makes sense to one may be aggravating to others. People try to understand their work, friends, and others and an organization's procedures and tactics in the face of evolving technologies and planning. While this may be helpful, rationality may not work.

Some human behaviors work against rational and mathematical logic. As G. K. Chesterton stated, "The real trouble with this world of ours is not that it is an unreasonable world, nor even that it is a reasonable one. The commonest kind of trouble is that it is nearly reasonable, but not quite. Life is not an illogicality; yet it is a trap for logicians. It looks just a little more mathematical and regular than it is; its exactitude is obvious, but its inexactitude is hidden; its wildness lies in wait."[5]

## DECISIONS ARE DIFFICULT

What happens when individuals cannot determine a logical definition of an issue or its solutions and, in some cases, even options for addressing it? In many cases, determining the upsides and downsides of possible decisions is not easy or even done, resulting in being frozen in indecision. In the historical past, people rested on the decisions of priests and other perceived wise individuals.

In disorderly and uncertain times, some leaders rely on their intuitive feelings. People who are familiar with an organization and environment may have a greater understanding of its people and circumstances than newcomers. Experience in problematic situations and knowledge of organizational culture provide a better foundation for intuitive decisions in times of disarray.

Decisions involve logic and brainpower, but also emotion. Sometimes logic and emotion collide. "I know what I should do, but my heart isn't in it." One's heart and emotions direct decisions, particularly in personal issues, but also at times in business or organizational life. Immeasurables are a part of life; not everything is measurable. There are no meters for love, curiosity, or commitment. How different people feel love is not measurable. Heartfelt issues have no way to be measured.

Leading in times of crisis or violence is particularly difficult. A superintendent in a midsized school district reflected on the circumstances of the shooting and killing of a principal of the high school during the school day.[6] He stated, "That crisis was absolutely overwhelming. Students were locked down in classrooms. It was around 2:12 when I was notified. We didn't know who shot the principal and whether or not the person was still in the school. The lockdown lasted until after five o'clock in the afternoon."

The superintendent indicated that he instantly clicked into a very rational and nonemotional pattern of thought in working with police, as well as in communicating with staff and parents at the particular school and across the entire district.

He said that "my focus was totally on what had to be done in the immediacy of this horrendous situation and protecting the children and staff, as well as ensuring that the other schools were safe." Only days and weeks after the tragedy was he overcome with the emotion of those moments. "I stayed focused on the responsibilities at hand to ensure safety, and never recognized the extent of the emotional intensity I or others experienced."

Reality can cause individuals to overlook their own feelings and emotions. Looking outwardl and not inward at oneself is necessary in times of leadership. As a psychiatrist working with the school district and staff concerning the killing said to the superintendent, "Why don't you come and talk?" The superintendent replied, "No, that's okay. I am fine." The psychiatrist replied, "You took care of everyone during this crisis but yourself. You are not okay!" The psychiatrist was right. The superintendent left his job ten months later and was divorced a year later.[7]

Not many of these highly volatile, emotional, and emergency situations occur in leaders' or others' lives. But there are lessons. Logic and reason are invaluable in life to analyze circumstances and make sense of things. But emotions are powerful, and their impact may not always immediately be evident.

The perception of some is that emotions are a negative condition in making decisions. However, ambivalence is really a major negative aspect of decision-making. In examining issues rationally, emotions will be present in evaluating options and developing a commitment, even if the final decision goes against self-interest. Context, time pressure, and relevance are important issues in determining the appropriateness of decisions.

## IMPORTANT LIFE DECISIONS

Everyone faces decisions. Some are inevitable, like careers, relationships, or commitments, and some are complex, carrying heavy content and deep impact. Others may be more trivial and personal. There are those decisions people are proud of and stand out as positive markers in their lives. And there are other decisions they regret. All people experience both.

Some decisions take thought and reflection, while others may be made or have to be made quickly or immediately. Crises often demand decisions without having all of the facts or details. Things may unfold slowly, but the prime factors in the situation are the safety of lives and the security of people.

Safe environments and facilities are important. Personal, family, social, and institutional security can be at stake.

Decisions are not of the same dimensions. Investments, purchases, personal interests, or connections may not be of deep magnitude. Person-to-person relationships, particularly socially, are of concern.

As people look back on decisions, they may be pleased or disappointed. Many times, individuals are indifferent to a decision or its outcome—it may not be that important or is routine. However, regrets can come from decisions as people look back on them through a different or broader realization of their importance and effect. It is not unusual for a parent to regret a decision. "Regret is a negative emotion you feel when reflecting on best decisions and wishing you had done something differently."[8]

Adrian Camilleri's research included 657 Americans between the ages of twenty and eighty.[9] He asked them about the ten biggest decisions they made in their lives so far. Some of these choices are to be expected—getting married, having children, starting a new job, obtaining a college degree. Less common were decisions about an unborn child or a dying parent. Concerning their own decisions, participants in the study indicated they had regrets.

In another study of 270 Americans, the six most commonly reported regrets involved romance (19.3%), family (16.9%), education (14.0%), careers (13.8%), finance (9.9%), and parenting (9.0%). Regret most often resulted from a decision "that moved you further from the ideal person that you want to be."[10]

In the book *The Top Five Regrets of the Dying*, author Bronnie Ware noted that the regrets stated most often were "I wish I . . .

- had the courage to live a life true to myself, not what others expect."
- didn't work so hard."
- had the courage to express my feelings."
- stayed in touch with my friends."
- let myself be happy."[11]

Life decisions are personal ones that individuals make that affect the quality or happiness of their life. Being related positively with others and being true to oneself are important—not simply playing a role or trying to meet the expectations of others. Making decisions for oneself and having the courage to pursue them elevates life and its value not only for oneself but also for others.

Decisions have to be made in all circumstances. Some are made quickly without time pressure. Fear and time can be great issues, and cognitive understanding and logic are the means. These decisions many times involve situations and circumstances that need to be analyzed and assessed.

People, as well as institutions and corporations, have these planned in systematic decision-making profiles. Analysts and experts are party to these decisions. Examples include meetings about retirement, fiscal factors, and organizational issues. School leaders experience and review curriculum additions or exclusions.

Immediate issues can be difficult, raising concerns and emotions and creating anxiety. These decisions are part of life and are like bumps in the road. Things break down, trips have to be canceled, and disagreements happen with loved ones or significant others. They are the bumps in the road affecting relationships, finances, or opportunities. In life, everything does not go according to expectations or plan. For example, errant happenings—getting a cold or receiving a phone call from your daughter's teacher—disturb the regular order of things.

Sadness and fear also erupt, creating major issues in personal or professional life. Job loss, family deaths, accidents, and other life-threatening events can rearrange issues and cause substantial distractions and disturbances, emotionally, cognitively, and physically.

In these times, emotions run hot, and attention to other aspects of life falters. At times, being present in the moment is difficult because emotional fear curtails rational analysis and clear thought. In these times, relationships are important, and the ability to depend on friends and loved ones is necessary.

Time is necessary to address emotions, but also to determine the content and the course of action. Major issues in life generally affect others as well as oneself. Adults in many cases feel responsibile for addressing concerns and finding solutions.

Sometimes things become complex, and issues of right and wrong are not the dilemma. Frustration grows when defining moments entail several "right" decisions. There may be two or more ways of resolving the issue, but there is no way to do both. Which choice does one select? Both are ethical. Both have similar consequences. Both are complicated, and similar ethics are involved in each. These "right-versus-right" moments, according to Joseph Badaracco, are defining moments because they reveal basic values, the commitments of people to the organization and others, and they shape the character of leadership and the organization.[12]

Leadership is not easy. The world and organizations are chaotic. People are not machines; they are living systems. Machines are equipment that complete a designated role or function. They make work easier; they have discrete parts with a specific function.

People are more complicated. They exist in a living system in which they must evolve, learn, and adapt to circumstances. Even in chaos, order emerges: focus on the whole, integrate work and activities, and examine systems.

Organizations are living systems where people work together to achieve a purpose that is significant and really matters.

Organizations and the people in them must have knowledge and understand how it is created and how it operates in a social setting.[13] Individuals must focus on the whole, not parts, and understand the necessity for integration of interactions. Finally, emphasizing the fact that the organization is a living system and not parts or pieces of a puzzle is essential.

## NOTES

1. Jeremy Sutton, "Erik Erikson's Stages of Psychological Development Explained," PositivePsychology.com, August 5, 2020, https://positivepsychology.com/erikson -stages/.

2. "The Decision to Drop the Bomb," USHistory.org, https://www.ushistory.org/ us/51g.asp.

3. Joseph L. Badaracco, *Defining Moments* (Boston: Harvard Business School Press, 1997), 47.

4. Lorenz, Edward, *The Essence of Chaos* (Seattle: University of Washington Press, 1995).

5. G. K. Chesterton, *Orthodoxy* (Overland Park, KS: Digireads, 2018), 55.

6. Anecdote source: Author, George Goens, *Superintendent of Schools*, Wauwatosa, WI.

7. Anecdote source: Goens, *Superintendent of Schools.*

8. Adrian R. Camilleri, "I Asked Hundreds of People about Their Biggest Life Decisions. Here's What I Learned," *The Conversation*, February 28, 2021, https: //theconversation.com/i-asked-hundreds-of-people-about-their-biggest-life-decisions -heres-what-i-learned-154885.

9. Chesterton, *Orthodoxy, p. 24.*

10. Camilleri, "I Asked Hundreds of People about Their Biggest Life Decisions."

11. Bronnie Ware, *The Top Five Regrets of the Dying* (Carlsbad, CA: Hay House, 2012).

12. Badaracco, *Defining Moments*, 6–7.

13. Peter M. Senge, *The Fifth Discipline* (New York: Currency Doubleday, 2006), 268–71.

*Chapter 3*

# How Did This Happen?

I do not enjoy Herr Hitler's acquaintance. He is living on the empty stomach of Germany. As soon as economic conditions improve, he will no longer be important.

—Albert Einstein, 1930

As long as I have any choice in the matter, I shall live only in a country where civil liberty, tolerance, and equality of all citizens before the law prevail.

—Albert Einstein, 1933

Decisions affecting people's lives occur at various levels and times. Some are not simply of their own volition. Others are the sole responsibility of individuals or the duty of a family, group, or others. Social decisions are made in a much broader venue of organizations, society, and government.

Behavior activates decisions based on personal, social, or professional responsibility, which carries duties and knowledge. So-called smart decisions certainly involve intellectual and personal skill, including information and data, emotional understanding, and obvious and intangible factors that influence outcomes.

In decision-making, responsibility requires having knowledge and the ability to analyze circumstances, data, conditions, and perspective, in order to draw conclusions based on information, as well as having intuitive and immeasurable conditions and attitudes. From these come actions and attitudes. Actions sometimes maintain the status quo or move in new directions. Timing must be right to get people's attention, understanding, and action.

Decisions require solid information that also includes values and beliefs. Judgments in all venues and circumstances must be based on information and analysis in order to define the possible outcomes, both positive and negative, as well as the unknown. Getting desired results necessitates achieving them in a moral and ethical manner. Some decisions are based on positive philosophy and concern for humanity, and others formulated for power and personal or professional gains.

Decisions carry moral and ethical consequences for individuals and organizations. Such decisions for society carry great weight and significance compared to routine or inconsequential options. Individuals examine their own lives and those of family members when making decisions. But there are large issues and decisions that can have positive, negative, or uncertain repercussions.

In any decision at any level, there are things that individuals, groups, organizations, and governments have the authority to do. In these situations, uncertainty and confusion may abound. In some cases, individuals may not even perceive that an issue exists. Others may think that it is of little significance, and some conclude that it is of no or little concern or that they have no power to address it or that it is beyond their scope or interest. Many feel that it is the responsibility of others. However, they may be expected to stay docile or may feel threatened if they do not go along or express their viewpoint or opposition.

Determining the truth is not always easy. People have biases. Some rest on opinion or prejudice. While the truth is fundamental in a democracy, it can be challenged. And half truths, irrelevancies, propaganda, deception, and formal and informal power exist. Falsehoods and inaccurate or deceitful research and conclusions can appear scientific and yet be inaccurate or spurious. Today there is a penchant to use statistics to influence others through numerical data or because of the speculation that data and research are accurate—which is not necessarily true.

Propaganda is evident in many social, political, or marketing situations. Propaganda is far from objectively examining all aspects of an issue and determining the pluses and minuses of an issue or solution. Marketing and selling, as in commercials or sales pitches for products or services, are not intended to include all data and information but simply to gain people's support.

Data is evident in all facets of life. Many think that numbers do not lie; they seem factual and connected to methodological objective measurement. But numbers can lie.[1] Numerical data may not accurately define circumstances because the sample size may be too small or the analysis of the data incomplete or inaccurate. Social media statistics may indicate the number of followers but not necessarily their agreement on issues. Some people may follow a site or organization for reasons other than agreement. The who, why, what, and how in data collection are important questions. Data can be collected and analyzed inappropriately and reported for a deceitful purpose.

Issues concerning data can be problematic when it comes to their meaning and conclusions. Consider the following:

- Correlation, not causation: the assumption that variable A causes variable B may not be correct. A and B may simply be correlated and not directly related as cause and effect.
- Selection bias can be problematic because of the implication that some numbers come from a random sample when they do not. They emanated from a nonrandom sample. For example, data from the Internet can be skewed to the readership profile of the website or report.
- How data is presented is an issue. Graphics have to be accurate to really present data correctly and truthfully. Graphs, for example, can be easily manipulated by the formation of the left axis.

Data, to some, is more factual than written analyses. Data collection, assessment, and the timing and process for its collection are all factors that determine its credibility and usefulness.

An unexpected issue concerns unintended consequences. Individuals do not perceive or see them as issues. Sometimes data misrepresentation happens without intention or planning. There can be drawbacks or perverse effects that are totally contrary to what was intended and can result in making the issue worse.

During the Vietnam War, as well as in others, the "fog of war" obscured issues, purpose, and outcomes. What is true? What is manipulated? What is the real outcome? What is the valid and true story? Do numbers in war accurately reflect a true picture? Are there unintentional situations that affect decisions?

With technology readily available today, education, ethics, and values must be the premium means to assess truth of data and evaluations. Without trust and truth, governments, citizens, businesses, and nations can be deceived, resulting in tragic and immoral outcomes. History has demonstrated that established and well-educated countries—cultured, civilized, and principled—can fall into unprincipled chaos.

## HISTORY: THE UNEXPECTED

History is filled with the unexpected. A sense of unpredictability is part of living. Everyone experiences unexpected results in their personal life. Nations do, too. Historical moments appear sometimes with clear natural events, but others, through the force or residue of human behavior, can come along spontaneously. Events like these can happen and do happen in all countries.

Looking back, historians contemplate and identify the irrational and incongruent courses in a society's or a country's history and culture. Germany is a prime example. Historically, Germany was considered a country of thinkers and culture. Consider the philosophers and artists: Immanuel Kant's work in metaphysics, ethics, and epistemology; artist Paul Klee's influence through expressionism and surrealism. Rainier Maria Rilke is noted as being a "lyrically intense" poet. Of course, Ludwig van Beethoven and Johann Wolfgang von Goethe hold highly distinctive positions in German music and literature. Karl Marx, philosopher and theorist, is also a historic figure for European and Western countries. All of these individuals are historic figures, influencing not only Germany but other countries across the globe to this day.

As a country, Germany was known for Christian values, literature, philosophy, art, logic, and reason. Strong family values were indicative of German culture. Respect for order and structure was characteristic. Society was portrayed as rule following, orderly, and completing things the right way. Citizens were direct, and they encouraged honesty, openness, and sincerity. But in Germany, history went wrong.

## NAZI GERMANY

History is complex and open to interpretation and change. History happens and events are not always positive. America and other countries have examples of poor decisions, immoral circumstances, and violence. How situations and circumstances evolve is open to conscience and effort but also influenced by emotion, beliefs, prejudices, and fear.

World War I provided some of the fodder for the turmoil that arose in the next twenty-five years. Germany's loss and the reparations and other political and economic circumstances emanating from the peace treaty had a damaging effect on citizens' outlook, leading to economic depression and social discontent. Adolf Hitler was an insignificant figure during and immediately after World War I. He mingled in beer halls, gave speeches, and floundered, wanting to become an architect.

The Nazi Party was focused on convincing German workers to reject socialism and communism. The party was a far-right, anti-Semitic, and racist organization. Originally, the party did not have great support, until the impact of the Great Depression.

The Treaty of Versailles imposed tough terms on Germany in 1919. The German monarchy was overthrown, and the Weimar Republic was instituted as a democratic entity. At this time, racism and anti-Semitism rose, with some Germans blaming the Jews and others for their defeat in the war. These right-wing groups were opposed to democracy, human rights, capitalism, socialism, and communism.

In 1919, Hitler attended a meeting of the German Workers' Party, which promoted national socialism. In 1920, the party's name was changed to the National Socialist German Workers' Party, which wanted complete obedience to the state and a racial struggle against Jews and "inferior races." Hitler wanted to unify all people of German blood.

He and his protégés attempted the "Beer Hall Putsch" in November 1923 in order to seize control of the Bavarian state. It failed, and Hitler was convicted and sentenced to five years in prison, but he was released after only eight months. During this time, he wrote his book *Mein Kampf*.

In July 1932, the Nazis became the largest political party, with 37.4 percent of the vote. After another election in November 1932, the Nazis were still the largest party, but with two million fewer votes. On January 30, 1933, Chancellor Hindenburg appointed Adolf Hitler as chancellor to form a coalition government.

As a result, Hitler persuaded Hindenburg to dissolve the Reichstag and announce new elections. With the February 27, 1933, fire in the Reichstag, civil liberties were abolished, and in the March 5 Reichstag elections, the Nazis obtained 44 percent of the vote. The Nazis were able to dictate laws without approval from the Reichstag or the president.

Hitler coordinated political parties, cultural institutions, and others in line with Nazi goals. Jews were eliminated from government agencies and economic, legal, and cultural positions. Trade unions were eliminated. The Enabling Law, passed on March 23, 1933, transferred legislative power to Hitler's cabinet. Hence, it became the foundation and source for all legislation and policy.

The Führer then guided all facets of life; authority flowed downward and was to be obeyed without question. Many Germans were ready for change due to unemployment, perceived national humiliation after defeat in the First World War, and the perception that the parliamentary government was weak and unable to successfully address the economic crisis. Many viewed the future through a darker lens, with greater economic turmoil and misery to come.

Hitler tapped into those perceptions and feelings through powerful speeches and propaganda that mobilized citizens who wanted action and change. The Nazis committed to German values, reversed the Treaty of Versailles, and stamped out the threat of communism. Blame for the economic and political situation corralled the fear and anger of citizens against the Jews, communists, and those responsible for the armistice in November 1918, as well as the signing of the Versailles treaty.

President Hindenburg's appointment of Hitler as chancellor of Germany was not done through a popular vote or mandate but through a deal of conservative politicians who gave up on parliamentary rule and hoped that, with time, the nation would return to conservative authoritarian rule. They were outmaneuvered, however, and a radical dictatorship was consolidated under Hitler's leadership.

In 1933, propaganda was the priority in Nazi Germany. Joseph Goebbels, the propaganda minister, created the Reich Culture Chamber. The arts are critically important in any society; they formulate and communicate values and principles, as well as history. The Reich Culture Chamber coordinated literature, film, music, radio, and theater. The fine arts and the press were also controlled by the Culture Chamber. The impact was that only artists and writers who belonged to the affiliated bodies could continue to create and produce artistic work.

The term *Gleichschaltung* was used for coordinating and synchronizing the remake of the Nazi state. All aspects of German creative, youth, and leisure activities were coordinated through Nazi principles. The *Kraft durch Freude*—"strength through joy"—program affected music, art, fitness, theater, and other programs.[2] This program and others were designed to ensure political, social, and cultural life was reorganized to serve Nazi goals.

The Nazi regime used propaganda very well to win the support of the population through the Ministry of Public Enlightenment and Propaganda. Stereotypes and images were used to influence the population and special interests. The propaganda machine was integral to the discrimination against Jews, fostering hatred and indifference to their fate.

The press control led all of this through mandates and instructions handed down from the government. Clause 14 of the 1933 Editors Law required editors to omit anything "calculated to weaken the state of the Reich abroad or at home."[3] Basically, the law enabled censorship of the press and publications. Journalists who failed in this were fired or sent to concentration camps. Editorial control by the government or any other group is extremely dangerous to free speech and to democracy.

The targeting of Jews, Romani, and others by the Nazis was perpetrated by Hitler and his collaborators, Himmler, Heidrich, and others, along with the SS. However, another pressing issue was the involvement of ordinary people, which contributed to the immoral and atrocious actions of the government and society.[4]

Questions and issues concerning common citizens and communities arise in terms of their responsibilities. The issue of "what did they know and when did they know it" comes up in legal questions and certainly international events that concern immoral and planned policies and actions of citizens and the government.

The Holocaust and its governance endorsed tyranny and raised these questions. While some in authoritative and powerful positions planned and instituted policies and procedures to eliminate a whole segment of the population, there were other "regular" and "ordinary" people who went about their work and daily lives. Doctors, lawyers, teachers, police officers, civil servants, and a vast number of regular citizens were "just doing their jobs," yet their individual actions resulted in human consequences far beyond one's imagination. Taken together, individual action can result in implications beyond understanding or measure.

Reviewing history and evaluating people's judgments and decisions seems easy, particularly when the subtleties of the larger forces are understood. What could the common person do with a government and society that are implementing decadent and immoral policies destructive to human beings and the nation itself? Looking back at Nazi Germany, it is hard to imagine people consciously subscribing to the destruction of millions of people through government policy and action.

After 1933, propaganda in Germany was tailored to different audiences. Many Germans were not Nazis and did not read party papers or follow events. Some citizens became National Socialists because of the issues of war, depression, and desiring change to address difficult circumstances. A woman who was active in a Nazi youth program stated, "I became a National Socialist because the idea of the national community inspired me. . . . What I never realized was the number of Germans who were not considered worthy to belong to this community."[5] Most Germans did not approve of anti-Jewish violence. But hard times and Nazi propaganda affected the general population. A majority of citizens were passive in their discrimination against Jews; people stood by as an increase in violence against them took place.

Germany engaged in activities contrary to democracy. It was not alone, as other nations pursued them as well. Book burning was a prominent activity—ironically so because Germany's culture emphasized philosophy, literature, and the arts. Free speech came at a human price.

The United States also confronted suppression of books in the 1950s. Senator Joseph McCarthy, who was concerned with communism, was alarmed at the availability of "subversive" books. Literature and books, as well as the arts, are considered dangerous by authoritarian figures because they can provoke people to question and think.

Many governments and societies perceive conformity as a positive attribute. Political control comes from the suppression of thought and philosophy. Hence, censorship becomes a national campaign to stop the spread of objectionable books and ideas.

Free expression is a basic foundation for democracy, creativity, and political and personal relationships. Without free thought, societies will be led by power brokers and dominated by personal interests, not by creative and principled individuals who look to the common good.

## HISTORY AND CONSEQUENCES

History unfolds slowly through relatively minor steps, and at other times change erupts in monumental sweeps. Speculation is always there, but what is of real consequence may come in small, innocuous steps. At times there are major, and sometimes overwhelming, decisions or events that almost instantaneously change history, but the full impact and weight on history is not always clear. Only in retrospect is the effect seen.

History does not always evolve through huge decisions. It happens through events and issues that at first seem inconsequential. However, they spur other events, some sequential in nature and others monumental in speed. The impact of decisions is not always quickly evident.

The values and principles behind decisions are of great magnitude. Maintaining honor, value, and standards is necessary in a democracy. The question arises whether or not positive values are part of life individually and collectively, and whether they are really understood.

Nations, like individuals, make collective and individual choices. Evaluating their premise and immediate and long-term effects is an absolute obligation of citizens. Our recommendations, proposals, and plans have both upsides and downsides. In every society and home, individuals must understand and define the benefits and hazards of proposals and decisions.

Personal and individual issues are more able to be understood because people are more likely to comprehend the options and consequences for themselves and others. Huge national and international issues are not always understood. The economic, political, and cultural issues that arise exist in a larger context that may or may not be easily understood.

Concerning national or international issues, appropriate questions and decisions are harder to contemplate and analyze. Citizens, even well-informed ones, are further from comprehensive understanding. People frequently rely on political principles and philosophy to guide their instinct, support, or opposition. Frequently, people follow political or cultural leaders and organizations to make decisions.

In addition, the greater context creates pressure and anxiety that would not be there if large economic or political challenges were not evident. In the case of Germany, the conditions stipulated that the end of World War I had a significant impact on later politics and perspectives. The end of the war, reparations, and the Versailles peace treaty were sources of condemnation.

Political parties sprang up, and Hitler and others used the outcome of the war and the treaty to build support. Hitler and the Nazis were not, by any means, universally accepted or taken seriously, but he had a passionate following.

The German economy fell into a tailspin, with unemployment hitting 24 percent. A new government was needed, and the choice for chancellor, with a balanced cabinet, was politically assigned. Hitler assumed power not solely on his own behavior but with the help of adversary politicians and German politics.

Hitler benefited from the larger issues of economic depression and conflict. The Nazis presented a posture of strength and a record of vitality that attracted people who did not vote before. A fatal perspective was that Hitler could be controlled and used for other politicians' broader agendas.

## CITIZENS AND DECISIONS

Every nation has a history that forms its decisions; some are based on the virtue of mankind, and others reject positive and moral principles. The United States and European, Asian, and African nations can look back and see the moral impact of their citizens, principles, and standards, as well as those of other nations around the globe.

National and personal histories are made on values and ethical principles. When the course is inappropriate, the decisions of citizens and the government can either establish a pathway to recognize the variance and change course, or subscribe to internal denigration and failure.

Citizens who stand on values and principles do not always receive accolades or praise. Historically, individuals have paid the price for standing up when the government and society take a course contrary to the concept of human values, liberty, and democracy.

Personal and civil decisions are very different in the authority and power to make them. Both have great responsibilities, but determining the direction is quite different. Personal choices are just that—authority and determination rest solely in the hands of an individual. Career, social, and family choices generally rest primarily on the control of individuals.

However, social and political decisions can be influenced by but are out of an individual's direct and universal control. They are made by legislative and executive governmental authorities at the local, state, and national levels. Citizens do have the ability to influence these larger institutions, but this requires a strong commitment to the responsibilities of citizenship. A major responsibility is to maintain a government structure in which citizens are active, not passive, cogs in the system.

In Germany in 1933, the shift to a totalitarian government in the aftermath of the Reichstag fire basically stripped citizens of power, moving authority into the Führer's hands. This was basically completed through consolidating power centrally without citizen or democratic control.

Citizenship requires comprehending and understanding what is actually happening. Thinking is necessary; seeing through propaganda is essential. Understanding democratic values, as well as those of totalitarianism, is essential; otherwise, citizens can fall into a herd mentality, driven by fear, propaganda, falsehoods, censorship, and suppression.

Truth becomes imperative. Citizens must be critical thinkers and question and determine whether policies and procedures are rational and unbiased. Evidence is essential to self-direct and evaluate analyses and policies. The Nazi occupation of Germany eliminated critical thinking, review of ideas, open communication, and dialogue and passed laws and pushed propaganda that incited bigotry, anti-Semitism, and eventually death camps.

Countries that suppress or distort the truth and curtail open discussion move to control and suppress thought and expression. History has demonstrated that in established democracies and new nations, truth is an issue, along with free expression, freedom of the press, and education versus indoctrination. In today's technological society, truth, expression, identification of sources, and control of expression are major concerns. The methods and forms of communication are formidable, and the control of expression is a major concern. The power of technology in producing or curtailing expression is very great today.

Standing alone in an authoritarian country is not easy and sometimes results in imprisonment or death. Concentration camps and reprisals by employers, neighbors, and local authorities make expression and debate very difficult for a person and his or her family and friends. Being silent and going along is the easiest way to protect oneself and one's family—but it can also be the next disastrous decision.

For dire circumstances like those in Nazi Germany, individuals look back and question what citizens knew and when they knew it. German citizens in other countries and agencies stood apart from the Holocaust. Once the regime gained power over all facets of the government, it was difficult for individuals to stand up and protest without suffering severe recourse.

A second category of bystanders includes German, European, and other populations who were passive or indifferent to events. Indifference is having a lack of interest in or concern about something—being apathetic publicly. Passivity implies inaction, which emanates from powerlessness, fear for safety, societal pressure, or lack of support.

In history, people have been indifferent to events and ideas. Indifference in many ways is destructive to humanity, principles, and truth. As Elie Wiesel stated:

> Of course, indifference can be tempting—more than that, seductive. It is so much easier to look away from victims. It is so much easier to avoid such rude interruptions to our work, our dreams, our hopes. It is, after all, awkward, troublesome, to be involved in another person's pain and despair. Yet, for the person who is indifferent, his or her neighbor is of no consequence. And, therefore, their lives are meaningless. Their hidden or even visible anguish is of no interest. Indifference reduces the other to an abstraction.[6]

## NOTES

1. Christopher Kim, "6 Ways Numbers Can Lie to Us," *Forbes*, August 8, 2013.

2. "*Gleichschaltung*: Coordinating the Nazi State," *Holocaust Encyclopedia*, https://encyclopedia.ushmm.org/content/en/article/gleichschaltung-coordinating-the-nazi-state.

3. "Ministry of Propaganda and Public Enlightenment," *Holocaust Encyclopedia*, https://encyclopedia.ushmm.org/content/en/article/ministry-of-propaganda-and-public-enlightenment.

4. "Law, Justice, and the Holocaust," *Holocaust Encyclopedia*, https://encyclopedia.ushmm.org/content/en/article/law-justice-and-the-holocaust.

5. "Defining the Enemy," *Holocaust Encyclopedia*, https://encyclopedia.ushmm.org/content/en/article/defining-the-enemy.

6. Elie Wiesel, "The Perils of Indifference," AmericanRhetoric.com, April 1999.

# Chapter 4

# Choices

We must consider the impact of our decisions on the next seven generations.

—Iroquois Confederation

The saddest aspect of life right now is that science gathers knowledge faster than society gathers wisdom.

—Isaac Asimov

All facets of life unfold through decisions by all social, economic, and political organizations, governments, and other institutions. The nature of decisions varies, and how to address them is dependent on type, timing, involvement, and other factors. Some decisions are informal and inconsequential and a part of daily life, while others are highly significant, substantial to current times or the future. Major decisions affect "life, liberty, and the pursuit of happiness" and the quality, direction, and success of individuals or institutions.

As people look back, they remember their best decisions and how they directed the course and experiences of their lives. Complex issues and their solutions are not always clear or obvious. There can be a variety of interpretations of circumstances and conditions, which are critical in assessing and evaluating situations. The nature of decisions and their implementation are key issues; the content may be correct, but the implementation may be problematic—or vice versa.

In all decisions, the depth of the issue in question is important in determining the content, who is involved, and the intention of the outcome. Consequential decisions carry the question of ethics and the process to be applied to outcomes. Ethics concerns not only issues of right and wrong but also the application of professional standards. Determining what is at stake and the appropriate ethical response is critically significant to the content, intent, and application of decisions. Professional and personal accountability are based on appropriate and ethical decisions and outcomes.

Every day, all people are affected by their decisions or those of others. Some of the consequences are routine, with little if any serious impact. Others have important or serious outcomes personally, socially, and professionally.

Decisions are made knowingly, but not always with a clear understanding of the circumstances, outcomes, or side effects. Decisions made by others—professionally, socially, politically—can bring major issues, opportunities, or difficulties.

At times, people decide not to make a decision and let things be. The decision not to make a decision is also a decision to let things flow. All decisions have consequences, some known and others surprising or unexpected. Hence, the attitude and perspective can vary from agreement to disagreement to antipathy.

Another important issue is how to react to the decisions of others, which is part of the communication process. Of course, not everyone has the background information to assess the quality of a decision. But decisions about decisions must be made anyway—sometimes on the basis of the reactions of others or the emotions of the issue. Emotions often play a role in formulating a response.

Decision-making and analysis require intelligence, information, perspective, and skill, along with strong character and principles. Too often people rush to judgment and do not have the necessary information and knowledge to evaluate the true nature or quality of decisions and their consequences.

At times, fear motivates reactions to decisions as well as the principles that underlie them. The consequences of decisions—known and unknown—are the critical elements at the core of every decision. The impact of these, which is sometimes speculative, affects tangible gains or losses, as well as the strength and competence of relationships and circumstances.

## LIFE DECISIONS

Each person has significant choices and personal standards for their options and how they live their lives. Leaders must decide, at times, whether they are the right person to make decisions or should rely on experts or others.

Do leaders have the knowledge, understanding, and skills required? People need to know their limitations concerning capability and comprehension. Sometimes a person in a business or an organization is not essential or needed to make or address some issues; other staff members or processes may be better qualified.

Focusing on more impactful decisions is what leaders must do. They do not have to do everything, which makes the role more difficult because it requires a conceptual understanding of the issues and complex decision-making processes and ability. Sometimes leaders must rely on others for information and decisions.

Timing is another issue. What is the best time to make the decision? Frequently, leaders feel pressure to decide quickly, to be decisive, which itself comes with hazards. Critical information may not be available, issues may not be clear, resources may be scarce, or other dynamics may subvert the process and the outcome. Timing can be as important as the issue itself.

Not including a person in the process, not taking a phone call, or not informing others on the scope of the decision can sabotage its effective implementation. Small factors—butterflies—can have a huge effect on decisions and their success.

Several issues direct a person's behavior and thinking about decisions.[1] These issues have an impact on the process, as well as the options and choices. They are reflective, in some ways, of the person's style and approach to issues.

Some leaders and others are impulsive. They react quickly and leverage the first analysis and option presented to them and do not allow time for greater discussion or input into the process. Sometimes the issue at hand requires a quick decision—timing is critical. This is often reflected in emergency circumstances, where quick decisions are essential to safety and survival.

At times, compliance and delegating are essential, but if these are used too regularly they can demonstrate a lack of decisiveness or courage on the part of leadership. However, to delegate requires trust in individuals, processes, and ethics to follow through on content, action, and values.

Weighing the positive and negative aspects of decisions is attributed to Benjamin Franklin. The intention is to think objectively in order to perceive the positive and negative ramifications of the decision. This process takes a bit more time than others, and not everything can be quantified.

Obviously, values are an essential aspect of decision-making because they help ensure better ethical, principle-based choices. Frequently, they can move the process faster because of the focus on values. Decisions can spur motivation because individuals feel positive about them and their supporting values. These decisions often highlight character. Principle-based decisions illustrate the wisdom of leadership in pursuing and sustaining important standards and values. Integrity in both reflects on the character of leaders and others.

Decisions confront people every day, and some may be very challenging. Prioritizing decisions is important and requires thought and even consultation to identify obvious and subtle aspects. A major issue is identifying the decisions that require immediate attention and consideration, while some are repetitive and innocuous.[2] Timing is an important concern. Many individuals have stated that "the issue would not have absorbed so much attention and time if I had acted faster."

Having individuals to whom one can delegate questions and issues is significant in organizations and institutions. Larger issues may require specific and specialized expertise beyond the scope of one person. Specialists with knowledge and understanding can provide insight on the knowns and also on the possible unknowns that may arise. People with appropriate knowledge and experience who have faced the same or similar issues can be great assets to leaders.

Being able to rely on people with proven capability and who clearly express the pluses and minuses of decisions is invaluable. Different viewpoints and approaches to decisions and goals are important to ensure all of the bases are considered and covered.

Decisions demonstrate and define values. Prior to making significant judgments, identifying the desired formal and informal outcomes and specifying the desired values for the process and goals of the decision are critical. People's reputations and characters are shaped by outcomes and the process used to achieve them.

Obviously, not all decisions are correct or implemented in an appropriate or timely manner. Some fail because of poor analyses or approaches that are inappropriate and not implemented in a timely manner. Decisions are not simply having goals and acting to achieve them. There is more to them than that. Philosophy is also involved.


## PHILOSOPHICAL MISTAKES

In life and decisions, there are viewpoints and matters of implementation for processes and approaches. According to Mortimer Adler, there are matters of subjectiveness and relativity, as well as objectiveness and absolutism. Everyone has heard individuals state that they want facts, not subjective opinions or desires.

Knowledge of facts and figures is one thing, but issues arise concerning moral values, what is "good and evil, right or wrong, with what we seek in our lives, and what ought or ought not to be done."[3] When individuals think something is really good, they feel it should be pursued. If individuals feel something is right to do, they think it ought to be done.

Some individuals feel that moral judgments are simply opinions and preferences. Arguing this assertion is difficult because challenging opinions often rests on the idea that it is useless and pointless because these judgments are pure speculation and beliefs. For others, there are clear matters of right and wrong. What is acceptable and what is not? They feel their position is incontrovertible.

Both positions are equally dogmatic and perceived to be subjective. Objective decisions are perceived to be impartial and unbiased. Relative positions are those that alter because of changes in circumstances. The issue arises about whether or not moral values and perspectives are dependent on the person's perception; personal values and judgments can be subjective or relative. Judgments about right or wrong, good or bad, just or unjust are moral or ethical judgments.

Not all decisions are going to be on the mark. It is important to learn from mistakes and content, emotion, presentation, professionalism, and timing. Learning from errors and poor assumptions can deter future problems and open doors to remediation.

## ASSESSING CONDITIONS

Decisions are more complicated than some believe or think. The issues and contacts are a bit more complex than deciding whether or not to have coffee in the morning. Practicality is involved, but so is philosophy. Individuals certainly examine the external context and the people involved. However, they seldom check themselves. After all, decisions made by leaders or individuals have a basic issue—themselves. Books on decision-making examine context and the concepts involved. But a key issue is also the person making the judgment.

A major issue is for the decision maker to be aware of what is in their mind. Events raise issues about the decision maker: what they are thinking. Emotions are present, but so are issues greater than simply feelings. Individuals have ideas and perceptions, as well as imagination, dreams, thoughts, concepts, and experiences.[4]

People's perceptions emanate from their life experiences and significant others. Individuals must distinguish between perceptual thought and conceptual thought. Conceptual thought involves connecting abstract and contrasting ideas to deepen understanding and possibly create new approaches. It also involves reflecting on past decisions and connecting ideas to improve future outcomes.

Perceptual thinking and interpretation of issues or sensations is based on one's experiences and specific context. This type of thinking is often called concrete thinking; interpretations are made through one's experience.

Knowledge is far more than opinion. Too often individuals selectively pick words or ideas to influence people. Individuals or companies try to place values and ideas to convince others to follow their opinion or position. Some use moral values to falsely gain support.

Finally, when it comes to choices, a basic tenet is essential: The critical distinction is between wants and needs. All individuals have basic needs for life. Some of the most obvious are food, housing, health, affection, and care. But we can go further: Artists need to create; professionals require the application of knowledge, skills, and talent in their area; parents require the ability to care for and love their children and family; and others, like teachers and police officers, want to contribute to society and their communities.

How people perceive the world affects their decision-making. Obviously, with responsibility comes decisions, whether in the workplace or at home. In some of these locations, it takes persistence to stay the course. Setting a course of action and adhering to it and seeking more information or wisdom may be necessary. In these situations, individuals have to accept responsibility.

Sometimes a decision requires holding others responsible for their choices. Seeking knowledge and pursuing wisdom are required in some circumstances. Compassion is necessary, but compassion in many cases requires dealing with the anger and resentment of others. Emotions rise under the pressure of circumstances, which can be overwhelming physically and socially. Individuals have to break free of fear and doubt because integrity rests with those making the decisions.

In personal or professional life, decisions come in several categories. Not everything is life or death. Some decisions are programmed and require a standard procedure. Some of these decisions are followed through organizational regulations or negotiated contracts. Routine and strategic decisions often concern operational procedures and goals.

In other cases, tactical decisions are necessary to manage the organization on the basis of solid policy and day-to-day activities. In many cases, middle managers and others make these decisions. Personnel decisions can be in this category as the organization functions and moves along in its day-to-day operations through procedures and policy.

Major decisions—concerning finances, operations, and politics, among others—are made at the top of the organizational structure. These decisions concern policies and goals, along with long-term financial planning and procurement.

While routine decisions are generally about daily operations, policy decisions require top leadership, legal counsel, and research. Routine decisions can be programmed, while policy decisions require legal and professional knowledge and control.

## LEGAL DECISIONS

The United States and other countries have a legal process for resolving conflicts and competing rights. While the legislature considers issues and passes laws to address them, the judicial system provides a means to challenge those legislative decisions. What is in the purview of the law and what is not, based on legal interpretation of the Constitution and corollary statutes?

The legal system establishes the means to make decisions on the appropriateness of a decision based on constitutional standards and the rights of individuals. Rights are stipulated in the standards, and processes are defined by the Constitution and legal precedents.

To determine constitutionality and individual rights, a court uses court-based facts and legal and constitutional standards. The decision is made independently on its merits and on meeting constitutional and legal standards and rights. Standards, rights, and legal authority are the bases for legal judgments and decisions. Third-party experts (lawyers and judges) make decisions on the question at hand based on compliance with constitutional standards.

Legal decisions in court are based on a rational model. The case must be based on facts, precedents, standards, and principles. Constitutional rights and precedents are the basis and are affirmed in the courts.

In all decisions, whether at home, at work, or in court, the individuals involved must understand the content and subject matter, as well as the organizational structures where the circumstances occurred. Decisions require the ability to analyze the policies and objectives at hand, as well as the alternatives available and considered. The time frame of decisions and the situation are also relevant; the pressure of time to decide issues affects the depth and pertinence of action.

Decisions require examining alternatives and their impact on formal and informal responses and ramifications. Getting insight from those involved is important because they can identify possible consequences and alternatives. Leaders and others must remain flexible in their thinking and analysis. Subtleties can become major issues as events unfold. Changes may be necessary as analyses become more sophisticated or thorough and reactions from key players become clear and evident.

Impacts and chain reactions may require reconsideration. Complex circumstances and issues require consistent review and thought. Life exists in a chaotic system with underlying patterns. Small changes can result in significant impacts.

Professionals in every domain make or are responsible for decisions. Top leaders require the cooperation of people throughout the organization concerning leadership, management, implementation, and supporting roles.

Department heads and other professionals in implementation and supportive roles are important in providing perspectives and insights about the limitations of decisions. Goals must have solid and beneficial strategies, along with confidence and trust, which will result in success and benefit.

Decisions emanate from choices made from analysis, planning, and evaluation. Not all results of decisions are necessarily desired. Sometimes goals are totally met, and at times they are surprisingly successful and open doors to greater progress, insight, and solutions.

As discussed earlier, rational decision-making models profess certainty and the ability to reach goals through selecting the optimal choice. The process is similar to the one discussed earlier: define problems, examine options, evaluate alternatives. Then make a decision, implement it, and evaluate its effectiveness.

A major decision is identifying the problem. Without doing so, time and energy will be squandered. Determining what is not the problem is also beneficial because time and focus are not wasted.[5] In many ways, this is the most important step, so that the right problem is defined and its priority is clear. If this is not done, generating alternatives to address it will not be accurate or beneficial.

Alternatives may or may not address the issue, or they may not be feasible or have the proper impact and influence on people. Generally, there is more than one solution or option to address the situation. The question is which ones really address the issue and at what cost to people and finances. At times, several solutions may be viable. Choosing the one that addresses the problem and has strong ethical support and professional basis may become clear.

Implementing a solution must be done accurately and clearly. Mediation with staff and others should be precise, and leaders must listen to and encourage individuals and the plan's implementation. This requires adequate funding, time lines, and clear responsibility for assignments.

With any problem-solving venture, evaluation of the process and outcomes must be conducted. In success, analysis, solutions, and outcomes meet desired goals and plans. Failure in meeting these goals and outcomes must be assessed. Was the definition of the problem wrong? Was the evaluation of its success or failure poorly defined or implemented? Were the right people assigned to lead and implement the plan? Proper definition of the problem is absolutely essential. Otherwise, time, effort, and resources will be wasted.

In some cases, particularly in highly publicized circumstances, leaders may not make the best decision but will settle for less. Sometimes, leaders decide to make progress on an issue because they do not have the full information or do not want to risk total failure of the issue in question.

# NOTES

1. Joel Hoomans, "35,000 Decisions: The Great Choices of Strategic Leaders," *Leading Edge*, March 20, 2015.

2. Hoomans, "35,000 Decisions."

3. Mortimer Adler, *Ten Philosophical Mistakes* (New York: Simon & Schuster, 1985), 108–16.

4. Adler, *Ten Philosophical Mistakes*, xvi–xvii.

5. Fred C. Lunenburg, "Decision Making Process," *National Forum of Educational Administration and Supervision Journal* 17, no. 4 (2010): 1–12.

# Chapter 5

# Character and Decisions

Every human person is inevitably involved in two worlds: the world they carry within them and the world that is out there.

—John O'Donohue

Success, like happiness, cannot be pursued; it must ensue, then it only does so as the unintended side of one's personal dedication to a cause greater than oneself.

—Viktor Frankl

Personalities differ in how they confront life because not everyone's perception is the same or seen through the same philosophical viewpoint. While we are all the same in terms of physical makeup, we differ in abilities and certainly personalities. No two people are the same in reality, even though they may dress identically. As most people understand, judging individuals by their physique, race, gender, or other physical factors or relationships is not accurate. There is more to people than their outer shell or perspective of them.

Individuals think, feel, and behave differently. Some are extroverts (social butterflies and outgoing) and others are introverts (shy and nonconformist). Some are open, and others more closed and reserved. Everyone has met individuals who are sensitive to comments and others who are thick-skinned or impervious to others' views or opinions.

Throughout life, most people meet very open people, conscientious individuals, socially adept, agreeable, or neurotic, frequently worrying and anxious about life and events. Obviously, some are closed, relaxed, energetic, quiet, and at times are seemingly distant and cold. The wonderful aspect of humans is that they can have a mix of these qualities. Some people who like to see tangible facts and figures, versus those who are intuitive and sense emotions and feelings. They both deal with making decisions but in different ways. Some use only hard data, and others apply their emotional feelings and intuition to direct their efforts. In many articles about leaders, these people are characterized as highly logical and following their reasoning, while there may be others who follow their hearts and beliefs. At times, problems are such that both rationality and heart are required; exceptional leaders are able to discern those circumstances, many of them having to do with ethical values and morals.

Everyone's personality is developed, in part, by the way they think. Some individuals are very logical and rational, and others are very creative and abstract. At various times, people may use all of these approaches; however, some professions require a particular type of thinking. Scientists require logical and rational approaches to thinking, as do physicians and lawyers. Obviously, writers, artists, and innovators may perceive the world differently and apply nonlinear and more abstract perspectives on life.

Individuals interact with others depending on how they think and respond to situations. Within each individual, people analyze and act on plans in order to reach goals and weigh consequences. In the process, they have to think deeply in order to make sense of what they perceive and determine the implications and consequences. Not all individuals perceive the world and events the same way.

Many times, people who are creative and innovative can be disruptive not only to their own lives but to the lives of others. Being creative and original is often pursued with great passion, which can be problematic. Many inventive people are driven to see beyond what happened. They can perceive subtleties and possibilities. Other individuals are only interested in focusing, understanding, and interpreting what they experience—the facts and figures. They accentuate immediate issues and are action-oriented concerning situations they face.

People do not approach issues or life the same way, simply because they were raised differently. Different times may call for different modes of thinking. Artists, scientists, and politicians perceive issues from individual perspectives. No one approach is better than the others.

Abstract thinkers are able to connect, at times, random things with each other. They see the big picture and make connections and search for meaning that may elude others. Problem-solving is a role they enjoy.

Analytical thinkers separate the whole into its component parts in order to see their relationships and use logic to find answers. Problems are restructured in a methodical way when examining the situation. Cause and effect are major concerns, not emotions.

Critical thinkers are quite analytical, evaluating and making judgments to determine the authenticity and accuracy of proposals or suggestions. They understand how to "make the case" and can judge things on their implementation and merit.

Creative thinkers, however, are out-of-the-box thinkers who can develop inventive ideas or solutions to solve problems and concerns or find new insights and approaches. Sometimes people do not take creative thinkers seriously because they can rattle the status quo and alter perspectives on standard analysis and solutions.

On the other hand, there are people who are concrete thinkers, opposite of the abstract ones. They like hard facts, figures, and statistics and approach thinking in a specific, not analytical way.

Some individuals are convergent thinkers, who look at a number of perspectives or ideas in order to find a single solution. They examine the possibilities and come up with what they consider to be the best resolution. On the other hand, divergent thinkers are the opposite of convergent thinkers. They explore an infinite number of solutions to find the one that is effective. They do not start off with a set number of possibilities but instead conduct a far-and-wide search to find a cause and a solution.

## PEOPLE AND DECISIONS

People confront many decisions in life. Many are routine, some are of personal significance, and others involve social, employment, and political spheres. Subjects cover a range of issues concerning personal desires and needs, relationships and family affairs, social and political situations, and employment, professional, and economic matters.

Not all people face the same questions, but all confront circumstances and matters concerning responsibilities, predicaments, and interests, determining personal and family relationships, and others that are distinct issues in people's lives.

In addition, no two people are the same. Their whole existence, while dealing with similar predicaments and quandaries, passions, tenor, and circumstances and situations, presents different conditions, narratives, and interactions. For example, difficult and confrontational relationships may be totally ineffective and inappropriate when having a thoughtful discussion around problems and solutions. Individuals may want a solution, but they have a personal need to vent their opinions and personal feelings toward others on the issue itself. While their emotional needs and reactions may be paramount at that time, they may desire a meaningful solution to the issue at hand.

While individuals may have a semblance of satisfaction with their lives, they may also have past desires or visions of what could have been in situations or relationships that never came to pass. Certainly, children have dreams and desires for their future, but so do adults. Even older individuals reflect back on their lives and hopes about how their lives would have been today if they had followed those desired courses.

Many people associate meaning simply with cognitive processes and desires. Life does fulfill the desire for meaning through intellectual pursuits and values, but it also resides in relationships, professions, and work by putting principles over personal recognition and wealth. A moral outlook on life and relationships places human life and fulfillment above recognition or fame.

However, people are driven by needs, some of which involve their need for self-esteem. Abraham Maslow indicated that all people have esteem needs.[1] He showed that individuals require and desire a stable, positive evaluation of themselves for their own self-respect and the respect of others. Individuals want and need this in confronting the world and issues with some semblance of independence and freedom. Reputation, recognition, and esteem from others are necessary for their own self-image.

Self-esteem, Maslow indicated, influences feelings of self-confidence and capability in confronting the world and its challenges. These feelings and experiences lead individuals to fulfill their potential and satisfy physiological, safety, affection, and esteem needs. Individuals can then pursue life creatively and to its fullest.

With one's ego, shame and anxiety are detractors because the ego wants endless recognition, success, and appreciation. Individuals feel that personal success is a measure of value. Fear of failure is a driving force. Consequently, individuals can live their lives chasing recognition from others or financial success, rather than committing to noble or ethical purposes.

## "DIE BEFORE YOU DIE"

The phrase "Die before you die" from Zen and Sufi spiritual traditions emphasizes the reality that each individual is going to die. In that vein, it simply means to come to terms with one's life and not sleepwalk through it. Examining life and its possibilities before it ends is a means to evaluate whether or not it is filled with one's potential and purpose. Is life focused on empty goals and activities that fill time but are not really noble or purposeful?

As the phrase "life is short" reminds us, each passing day, week, month, and year should not go by without fulfilling one's spirit, soul, and intelligence. Going along with others' expectations and goals will not feed the basic needs of all human beings. Life is more than material goals or popularity and certainly is not filled with meaningless activities and dubious desires.

Individuals are responsible for being aware of and alert to the real needs of their lives. They go beyond physical health and economic sustenance. Being true to oneself is important in order to understand life's purpose and what truly matters. Facing the fact that life eventually ends helps individuals focus on what is important. Life is truly mesmerizing and awe-inspiring. Reflect on history and one's experience and comprehend its purpose and impact.

What truly matters when all is said and done is that life was made meaningful because of intangibles. Life would be truly empty without love, truth, meaning, friendship, gratitude, happiness, compassion, peace, fullness, and freedom.[2]

## STRUGGLES

In much of contemporary society, prominent people, leaders, presidents, and others are presented and portrayed as individuals who succeeded because of their emotional and intellectual strength. Focus, knowledge, and intelligence are the keys to breakthroughs and consistent achievement. Their abilities are only exceeded by their optimism and concern for the common good.

But Hollywood portrayals and public relations gambits do not present leaders and officials as human beings with doubts and fears of their own. All-knowing and self-assured leaders are not the reality among people who have great responsibilities or pursue standards and principles. Leadership is not what entertainment vehicles or press reports make it out to be.

All people, including formal and informal leaders, confront important issues in their roles and must also deal with their personal concerns and doubts. Informal leaders are those who through their personal relationships and character are looked to by others for their knowledgeable viewpoint and direction.

Formal or informal leadership roles include responsibilities and struggles. Regular unexpected issues are prevalent in most roles and positions. Pressures around time and responsibilities generally come with the role or job. However, situations and circumstances present more than the expected in terms of duration, guidance, energy, and ideas. It is also important to structure responses to conditions and people. Some issues are the result of prior decisions, unexpected external influences, or emergency situations or occurrences.

Formal or informal leaders experience emotional weight and uncertainty, coupled with obvious and ill-defined challenges. Clarity of all issues and concerns is not always possible as things unfold and play out. With that come challenges and obstacles that create pressures around time, certainty, and emotions.

In some circumstances, difficult emotions are a factor and can run high. Anxiety to do the right thing grows and can, if not handled properly, distract leadership and detract from responding in a timely and correct manner based on principles, values, and professional norms. In addition, anxiety and tension make it harder to identify the true nature of the situation and the most effective responses to address major and associated issues, professionally and personally.

Leadership concerns addressing formal and informal challenges. Responses are assessed by individuals internal and external to the organization. Emotional turmoil can prevent making correct and timely responses. Doubts extend the process in terms of pressure and timeliness. People in leadership positions have three different styles in confronting major issues and challenges.[3] Not all of the roles are productive; sometimes leaders do not openly present questions and concerns in their entirety.

Some leaders take the "hero" role, focusing solely on the positive to convince teams that they will get through the crisis, no matter what the conditions. Positivity can improve performance, but leaders who ignore negative emotions can make people feel worse and fail.

Another style is that of "technocrat," which again focuses on tactical solutions to issues and problems. Both heroes and technocrats ignore emotions and their impact. Some leaders feel that citing emotion deters others from focusing on practices to resolve questions. In these circumstances, people strictly address actions and goals, which can result in creating distance between leaders and their staff. Maintaining a façade of positivity and ignoring emotions does not work in highly difficult circumstances. "While emotions may seem frivolous to some, they, in fact, drive everything leaders care about, from job performance to turnover to customer satisfaction. By ignoring emotions, technocrats fail both to harness the positive emotions that spur performance and to address the negative emotions that undermine it."[4]

All individuals need respect and concern. A major matter in relationships is acceptance, without which any honest interaction will not take place. People recede inside themselves and will not reveal their opinions and philosophy. Acceptance allows individuals to be open to other people and is liberating, freeing them to be who they are. The third type of leader, the "sharer," fosters this openness. Listening is essential, and through it comes mutual understanding, with each person responsible for the depth of their feelings, their mind, and their heart.[5]

Too often people only talk with individuals with whom they agree. Citizens cannot gain an understanding of the positions of others politically, socially, economically, or personally while only interacting with individuals with like opinions and philosophies. Comprehending differences and possible conflict and stress can lead not necessarily to agreement but to understanding. People want to be understood: agreement is not always helpful or possible, but being understood can open doors and relationships.

## THE COMMON GOOD

A major part of life is to realize that people have more similarities than differences. Categorizing individuals is destructive and vacant of any idea about life and understanding. It is a pathway to ignorance and contrary to opening connections and compassion.

Once again, human beings have more similarities than differences. Of course, not everyone thinks alike, has the same beliefs, or agrees on philosophy and principles. However, physical differences in age, size, strength, race, gender, or nationality should not create separation or discrimination. The same is true for an individual's philosophy—some interpret life, governance, and principles liberally, and others take a more conservative interpretation.

Understanding is different from agreement. Comprehending the position, values, and philosophy of individuals does not require endorsement or acceptance, just understanding and insight. A democracy is built on this concept because without it discussion and debate are futile and political and physical power become the standard. The common good requires citizens and others to respect differences to maintain civic order and democratic processes.

People frequently use the words *heartfelt* or *heart* when describing relationships and demeanor. Individuals sometimes use the phrase "In my heart I . . . ." Love resides in the heart. "In my heart, I know we are meant for each other." There is a gauge for assessing blood pressure, but not so for love.

Every individual has a self, which is where all of our ways of knowing converge— intellectual, emotional, sensory, intuitive, imaginative, experiential, relational, and bodily, among others.

In personal, political, or professional relationships, valuing differences is essential. Everyone is unique. Everyone has beliefs and experiences. Everyone has value and merit. Everyone has a unique character. Everyone's life is to be valued. In that regard, everyone is a distinctive individual, interpreting and living life based on their views, experiences, and values. Priorities are determined by them, their family life, and their needs.

Parker Palmer indicates that individualism should not become selfishness. He identifies five habits of the heart to sustain a democratic society. Understanding that "we are all in this together," we must appreciate others. Tension exists in society and in viewing one's life. Life is full of contradictions, and everyone needs a personal voice and agency. Finally, people should express their visions of truth, check them, and correct them as needed. In doing so, a sense of community can be achieved. "The heart is where we integrate what we know in our minds with what we know in our bones, the place where our knowledge can become more fully human."[6]

## LEADING

Leading is difficult. Anyone who has had to lead looks back on their role and performance. But in all honesty, mistakes and failure are part of leadership; good leadership requires insight and decisions in times of turmoil, insurrection, and uncertainty, confronting knowns, unknowns, and unknown unknowns.

Leaders look back and examine their circumstances, goals, actions, and decisions. In many cases, they review intense and highly difficult situations and their analysis and actions in dealing with them. Leaders, in particular, have high expectations for their actions and decisions. At times, they also have regrets.

Regret arises when we feel we could have acted more effectively or we second-guess ourselves in light of all the information that becomes available. When reviewing decisions, pressure is an issue. A study of older adults identified the regrets in life—professional and routine. They are relevant to all people, in or out of leadership positions. Common individual regrets include the following:

- Not living for their values and ambitions, but living for the expectations of others
- Working too hard and missing time with family and others
- Not having the courage to express their feelings
- Not staying in touch with friends
- Not allowing themselves to be happier

These issues have nothing to do with economic rewards or fame. They concern living life and meeting one's values and principles and maintaining relationships with others.

The major issue surrounding these regrets is living a satisfying life. A major concern is staying in relationships with others and not living in isolation. Social belonging is important for one's sense of acceptance and the closeness of friendships, personal relationships, or with those who are "polestars" in our lives.

A second issue is inaction. Many individuals look back and regret not pursuing interests, relationships, or learning. They regret dropping opportunities concerning relationships or romantic connections. People have concerns about lost opportunities, even when undesirable outcomes may have pervaded. Not trying leaves an emptiness that people wonder about. In some cases, these decisions may move an individual from the person they desired to be. Individuals' decisions, including not to decide, direct a pathway and the future.

## NOTES

1. Abraham H. Maslow, *A Theory of Human Motivation* (New York: Start Publishing, 2013), 14–15.

2. Maslow, *A Theory of Human Motivation*, 255.

3. Lauren C. Howe, Jochen I. Menges, and John Monks, "Leaders, Don't Be Afraid to Talk about Your Fears and Anxieties," *Harvard Business Review*, August 18, 2021, https://hbr.org/2021/08/leaders-dont-be-afraid-to-talk-about-your-fears-and-anxieties.

4. Howe, Menges, and Monks, "Leaders, Don't Be Afraid to Talk about Your Fears and Anxieties."

5. Ed Shapiro and Debbi Shapiro, eds., *Voices from the Heart* (New York: Jeremy P. Tarcher/Putnam, 1998), 302.

6. Parker J. Palmer, *Healing the Heart of Democracy* (Hoboken, NJ: Wiley), 43–44.

## Chapter 6

# The Pursuit

## *Meaning*

> Hope is a feeling that life and work have meaning. You either have it or you don't, regardless of the state of the world that surrounds you.

> —Václav Havel

People usually think of their life in an external way, examining what is outside of themselves as if they are bystanders to a play unfolding around them. People think the context is "out there" in the greater world, as if they exist solely in a social, political, and economic context. Certainly, our society, community, and institutions present issues that are a part of their existence. Life emerges in mysterious and engaging ways, pursuing challenges and prodding opportunities for finding meaning and living deeply.

If life was a flat line with no peaks or valleys, there would be little poetry in the nature of things. People live in the messiness of day-to-day life, with its emotional beats of the heart and soul and the clash of reality and principle that pull events and happenings.

In life there is an unseen world of forces and intangibles; the things that are hard to measure make people uniquely human and alive. Life is an emotional venture offering insight, wonder, creativity, and motivation. Hearts, minds, and souls are at play, far beyond the ability of artificial intelligence or other hard-nosed technologies that are bereft of imagination or emotion.

Introspection causes people to think about the meaning of life, the future, and their legacy. A legacy has nothing to do with fame or fortune. It is more personal than acclaim. It is more philosophical and not about recognition. What is meaningful in life for one person is not universal to others because meaning comes internally from their personality, philosophy, principles, perspective, and purpose. Creating meaning is quite personal. Material goods are vacant of emotion or feelings; affluence and materialism are not always significant to a fulfilling life.

Vickor Frankl reviewed his experience in a concentration camp in World War II, in which he experienced and observed tremendous suffering.[1] He concluded that those individuals who lived for something greater than themselves and had a purpose for their lives had a better chance of survival than others. People with a clear purpose were able to overcome difficulty and sadness. When people make sense of their lives, when they develop commitment and have a focus for it, they have something to live for. Individuals must live authentically and genuinely to find meaning and happiness by defining their ideals and principles and being clear about what is not negotiable in their lives.

Living a life just to accumulate material goods and money is hollow and will not bring happiness. People who live enthusiastically really use their talent and commit to their beliefs and values and find happiness and satisfaction. Happiness cannot be sustained without a sense of meaning. Living authentically and genuinely is the path to finding meaning. Being clear about ideals and principles and what is nonnegotiable in life is necessary for a rewarding path.

## LIFE

Most people express a desire to live a good life. But good has many definitions, depending on the individual's beliefs, philosophy, and values. Some people consider economic conditions to determine a "good" life. Others work toward defined goals, careers, and positions. Yet others in dire circumstances, in times of loss or difficulty, perceive those times as periods of growth and understanding. Even in horrible times, in the midst of concentration camps and losses, individuals grasp for a philosophy of life.

Generally, people do not think about the meaning of life. On the surface, they go about daily tasks, plans, and activities. Individual and family needs, along with employment and personal responsibilities, take precedence. The meaning of life generally does not surface in one's daily regimen.

Life, however, includes difficult and serious issues. Suffering, physically or mentally, or moral issues arise because of one's actions or inactions or due to social or economic circumstances. Meaning in life is not always easy. People at times feel contentment with their lives, but not necessarily deep meaning. There is no guarantee that everyone will find or understand the meaning of life.

American society is geared to satisfying everyone's needs through consumer diversions. Many people seek distraction and shred the capacity to engage in difficult or challenging things because of the need for instant gratification. Short-term gains or diversions may distract individuals, but they do not offer a sense of meaning in the end. As a result, some people ignore or neglect finding or participating in personally meaningful relationships or activities.

Meaning to some is an abstraction, a term frequently used but with little understanding. Some simply seek a life of material ends and affection. Searching for meaning and fulfillment has unexpected results far beyond materialistic self-gratification. In fact, it has impact far beyond status and materialism. The basic need for meaning is "important because once a man's meaning is fulfilled, he becomes able and capable of coping with frustrations and tensions, and—if need be—he is prepared to give his life."[2]

Living a life of meaning requires commitment to values and ideals in humanitarian and ethical circumstances. Truth is important, as are relationships based on care and affection. The love of ideals and people is important as a commitment and achievement beyond self-gratification. Authenticity in personal and professional lives is developed through clear and open commitment to issues and problems. Authenticity in life leads to satisfaction and happiness.

Each person's course through life and its stages is individualistic; some are clear and easy, and others cloudy and uncertain. In reality, no one can make other people's lives because each individual has autonomy over their values, needs, and capabilities. Every person has a need to create a life. In many cases, as children, people aspired to be athletes, to be famous musicians, to work in professions like their parents, or to be scientists, professors, politicians, or other professionals.

Everyone requires autonomy to create a life of their own. Some parents feel slighted if their children pursue a different job, profession, or lifestyle. Each individual needs to be their own person. "Life is born from this unquenchable need to be. One of the most interesting definitions of life in modern biology is that something is considered alive if it has the capacity to create itself. The term for this is *autopoiesis*—self-creation. Life begins from the desire to create something original, to bring a new being into form."[3]

Self-determination is a value of American culture. Independence involves the right to decide and learn to live with the uncertainty and chaos that life brings. Finding and pursuing meaning is a forceful motivation for individuals to create unique lives of their own. Life is exceptional and open to each individual to create it.

## FEARS

All people confront one basic question in life: Who am I? There's no getting around it because it dwells within them throughout life and its experiences and challenges. It is the most challenging question anyone confronts because it directs one's decisions and ultimately one's life. This basic question defines one's character and nature, including obligations and commitments. All individuals hope to know themselves in order to determine their sense of responsibility and how they traverse through each stage and role in an undefined life.

People need to determine how they approach their lives. Do they take personal responsibility for their past, present, and future? Do they persist and confront issues in a manner conducive to their values? Are they passive, dependent, or action-oriented? Do they seize the moment or defer because of fears or self-doubt? Do they know and understand what is in their heart? Do they forgive themselves for their errors and misjudgments? Do they forgive others? Finally, do they address each day or challenge in a grateful manner and with a happy and appreciative spirit for the challenges and opportunities they face?

People have fears, which can be detriments to achieving love or happiness—two emotions that cannot be felt simultaneously with fear.[4] Fear is powerful and can circumvent progress and block happiness and true feelings.[5] Fear can grow more fear, and very often love grows and expands love. Fear often turns into anger, and anger often circumvents growth as individuals fall into a cloud of anxiety.

Happiness resides in people's souls and hearts. Happiness is a positive state and depends on how individuals deal with what happens. How events are interpreted and perceived determines reactions. Often people feel that they do not deserve happiness. Too often people feel victimized. But difficult experiences and outcomes occur in everyone's life. Adopting a victim mentality is a recipe for failure. Emotions nurture and create one's perceptions of reality.

Difficult times bring distress and suffering. Life requires having to confront peaks and valleys. Through life's ups and downs and experiencing emotional, physical, and intellectual trauma, perspectives exist and the physical and psychological demeanor of individuals can result in growth and a greater understanding of life's purpose and meaning.

People who suffer loss—death, unemployment, relationships, or others—are given the opportunity to review and recalibrate their priorities and relationships. They can be "haunted by the experience of their inner emptiness." Frankl states:

By declaring that man is responsible and must actualize the potential meaning of his life, I wish to stress that the true meaning of life is to be discovered in the world rather than within man or his own psyche, as though it were a closed system. . . . The more one forgets himself—by giving himself to a cause to serve or another person to love—the more human he is and the more he actualizes himself.[6]

Meaning can be found in work, by accomplishing something, through experiences or encounters with others, or by the attitude one takes in the face of unavoidable suffering or difficulties. Many individuals focus on the darkness of life, but within difficult times can and do find nature and other individuals with whom they find love and acceptance. Loving another opens the door to introspection and self-assessment.

Suffering frequently means sacrifice, which transforms into meaning. History provides examples of individuals who engage in sacrifice, hardships, or distress that was necessary to save and defend principles or provide a better life for others.

Life evolves from birth to death and is filled with stories and experiences unique to each person. While similar events are expected in people's lives, what experiences and transactions become transformational rests inside the life and psyche, mind, soul, and spirit of each individual. Everyone has their own mission in life—everyone's life is unique. In many cases, suffering experienced produces the greatest pride and leads to satisfaction.

In tough and difficult times, things can be confusing and uncertain. Individuals can be thrown out of balance. Fear can drive people to frantic behavior and a loss of their sense of their role. They lose their mission and the fact they are interconnected with others and their mission.

In crisis situations, action may be required, sometimes without time for thought or reflection. Something must be done to get through the immediacy of the circumstances. The unexpected always happens in crisis situations, but what is necessary is strategic thinking to anticipate what possibly could unfold in order to apply foresight and to anticipate strategically. Applying principles and ethics in planning strategies and goals is necessary. Integrity to values is indispensable in leadership actions and reactions.

Crisis situations often result in defining moments. Leaders must understand the circumstances and place emotional distress aside to rationally work through the turmoil and save lives, reduce spinning out of control, and provide stability and confidence in a chaotic and fearful time.

In these situations, one's mind creates the reality, and at times this reality is not always rational. Emotions are powerful, and biases filter and influence an individual's reaction and actions. People, leaders in particular, must become mindful—aware of their thoughts and emotions.

Focus is essential so that objectives and strategy are maintained to reach goals. Leaders must stay in the present so they can notice what is happening and unfolding. They need a clear focus on what they are thinking and feeling. By doing so, conscious choices and clear, deliberate actions can be made.

Meaning does not just fall out of the sky, and it does not always mean winning. It is not one event or achievement, but is the composite of a continuous and often unpredictable deliberation between circumstances in life and the potential purpose individuals put to it. People discover things about themselves and others in this process.

Human beings learn from difficulty and sorrow. In many ways, these situations highlight the meaning of life. Sorrow and love are tightly coupled. Everyone has a unique life, with loving relationships, experiences, and circumstances all their own. Talent and skills honed through relationships, sacrifices, practice, and beliefs lead to decisions made with values and principles.

How did individuals get to where they are to understand and live life in a constructive and mature way? They learned that they, in many ways, are responsible for creating their own life and future. Accepting that responsibility is a major characteristic of maturity. In this process, individuals must deal with failure and know when to back off or intercede. There are times of independence and others of dependence.[7]

## HAPPINESS

So often people, especially children, think that happiness flows through winning, gaining position or titles, and of course money. Certainty, Madison Avenue and Wall Street pitch that prominence and finances are the pathway to success and a good life. In this light, recognition and physical accomplishment form the basis of a secure and happy life. Physical security is important in life, but happiness requires more.

Researchers have found that older people tend to be happier than younger ones because they focus more on remembering positive events, not the negative ones. By doing so, older individuals regulate their emotions to a greater degree than younger ones.[8] Elders do not have employment concerns and have more direct influence on the people with whom they associate. In addition, the challenges and responsibilities of raising children are not a daily part of their lives.

In essence, priority shifts for older adults. They realize that time is running out, which causes a change in priorities. "Older people think, 'Let's make the most of the time we have, let's optimize our emotional experience.' Older adults perceive time in life is growing more precious. They also have experience from time lived, so they know how to regulate their emotions by controlling their environments and minimizing their exposure to things that will upset them."[9]

As individuals age, there are different challenges. For older people, health is a major concern. But issues, though different, exist at all ages. As people move into their seventies, they more fully understand life and its course.

In essence, people begin to realize that happiness does not come from external sources. What one thought in younger years does not produce the desired contentment and purpose people aim for. Pleasure is one thing, but purpose is something else.

What is necessary is for people to become more aware of what makes them truly happy. Materialism and social recognition become blind alleys as people pursue fame, popularity, and fortune. Understanding at an earlier time in life that time is limited clarifies what is important and how time should be spent. Finding fulfillment does not come from driving to the bank.

All parents recognize times past when they had a special heartfelt moment with their child filled with love and warmth. Being true to one's values and staying in the moment are important. Those are times when one feels life matters and that one is connected to others beyond physical presence.

As Thomas Merton stated, "Finally I am coming to the conclusion that my highest ambition is to be what I already am. That I will never fulfill my obligation to surpass myself unless I first accept myself, and if I accept myself fully in the right way, I will already have surpassed myself."[10]

## NOTES

1. Viktor Frankl, *Man's Search for Meaning* (New York: Washington Square Press, 1984).

2. Viktor Frankl, *The Will to Meaning* (New York: Penguin, 1988), 167.

3. Margaret Wheatley, *Finding Our Way: Leadership for Uncertain Times* (San Francisco: Barrett-Koehler, 2005), 24.

4. Elizabeth Kubler-Ross and David Kessler, *Life Lessons* (New York: Scribner, 2000), 138.

5. Kubler-Ross and Kessler, *Life Lessons*, 143, 208.

6. Frankl, *Man's Search for Meaning*, 128–33.

7. John Gardner, *Living, Leading, and the American Dream* (San Francisco: Jossey-Bass, 2003), 55–56.

8. Association for Psychological Science, "Why Are Older People Happier?" *ScienceDaily*, January 12, 2012, https://www.sciencedaily.com/releases/2012/01/120106135950.htm.

9. Susan Bell, "Happiness Across the Lifespan: Not a Slippery Slope after All," *USC Dornsife*, November 25, 2019, https://dornsife.usc.edu/news/stories/3117/happiness-across-the-life-span-not-a-slippery-slope-after-all/.

10. Thomas Merton, *A Search for Solitude: Pursuing the Monk's True Life* (The Journals of Thomas Merton, vol. 3), May 1996.

# Chapter 7

# Crisis and Decisions

Everyone thinks of changing the world, but no one thinks of changing himself.

—Leo Tolstoy

I am a firm believer in the people. If given the truth, then they can be depended upon to meet any national crisis. The great point is to bring them real facts.

—Abraham Lincoln

While leaders and others think and plan for the unexpected and potentially dangerous and tragic events, when they occur, they are shocking, overwhelming, and volatile.

Certainly, the loss of life is a major crisis under all circumstances because it is the essence of being and love, and when a loved one is lost the pain affects individuals throughout their lives. Losing a parent at a young age is a lifelong loss of a relationship that resides only in memory. The depth is not always understood.

People find themselves in crisis situations when circumstances are obstacles to achieving their goals or solving problems. Often in these situations individuals cannot overcome the obstacles in the usual or customary ways, or they are overwhelmed and do not have a response to them. Being static or stuck creates distress and a loss of direction. In these situations, individuals may have a negative perspective of their ability to react and cope.

Being "frozen" in the face of distress or turmoil results in great pressure. Identifying options means addressing some aspects, lowering stress, and restoring some semblance of equilibrium and the ability to work through events. Some individuals change into a highly focused frame of mind, beyond the emotional shock and immediate disbelief that a death occurred.

In crisis situations, there is a threat to individuals' life stances and relationships. Sometimes surprise is involved because of an unusual or totally unexpected incident or event. Decisions often have to be made in short order to ensure the safety and security of others.

## CIRCUMSTANCES

*Crisis* is a word used for many circumstances and situations. Historically, the United States has faced financial crises in the form of depressions and technological transformations that altered employment, manufacturing, and communication. And nature has produced natural crises due to weather, climate, and pandemics.

Other crises involve physical confrontations and skewed values through deception, misconduct, or violence. Historically, wars, genocide, food shortages, and climate and weather emergencies have occurred. Some of these were created by human beings through political decisions, and others through acts of nature. Crises are part of life personally, nationally, and naturally. In these circumstances, decisions must be made by individuals, organizations, and the government, depending on the nature and scope of the situation.

Crises involve several issues that affect reactions and decisions. Whether in international or national circumstances or conflicts, there are some common variances. According to the Oxford English Dictionary, *crisis* is defined as "a time of great danger, difficulty, or confusion when problems must be solved or important decisions must be made."[1]

When making decisions, individuals require complete information. The problem is that, in a crisis, all the necessary data or evidence may not be available. Incomplete data and expertise are usually the norm in serious issues or crises. With incomplete information, it is wise to remember core values and principles in addressing the situation. Obtaining the advice of others who have knowledge and perspective is invaluable.

Timing is important because all facts and details, as well as implications, are not going to be clearly evident in these situations. Lives and safety matter, and immediate decision-making is critically important.

Crises always have knowns, unknowns, and unknown unknowns. Only in retrospect can all factors and forces be understood. Leaders, however, must act in the present as circumstances unfold. Historians can look back, but leaders must lead from a present that is changing and progressing.

When a crisis is unfolding, the number-one priority is the lives of people involved. Safety is primary. Metrics do not always accurately describe the situation. Lives involve more than cold, hard facts, and making decisions requires a priority be placed on the human imperative of decisions. Crises raise fears. Silence raises concerns. Some people become impatient, others will not do anything unless high levels of evidence exist for all groups, and other individuals will become highly emotional and unable to function.[2]

In all of these, reason and emotion are at play. Decisions are going to raise emotions, and cognitive analyses will be based on reason and logic. However, reason may not always be accurate. People can use the same logical thinking but come to a different conclusion. Some will say there is no logic. Interpretations of data and available information exist; however, in a crisis, all data may not be available or tangible.

The opposite of the word *logic* is *specious*, *unreasonable*, *irrational*, or *senseless*; however, a decision made on past issues or that is procedurally rational may not always be correct. Life is not always totally rational. When a decision is complex, knowing all of the elements and conditions involved may not be possible. Unidentified significant issues may be at work, as well as undetermined forces and pressures, organizationally, politically, and personally.

Organizational literature provides steps and processes to make rational decisions. The steps are clear. Identify the problem, review the various options, and then compare them to discern which is the most advantageous. In this process, there is the issue of decision makers selecting the decision most satisfying to them. Intuition may be at play in this routine.

Everything is not always evident when facing challenges and concerns. Economic, social, and personal attacks are present but not always evident, unless people compare options thoroughly and get the viewpoint of others. At times, leaders can get too close to the issue and need to get the intelligent and impartial viewpoint of others. Considering those viewpoints will help leaders assess their own impressions and see other possibilities that were not clear before. Fresh perspectives are helpful if time permits. Sometimes, however, emergencies require quick but thoughtful reactions. All data and information are not always available.

Some professionals rely on timely critical decisions. The military, for example, where life is at stake, has a seven-step process to define and make choices and pursue a course of action.[3] Obviously, the issue must be clear, and all of the variables that contribute to it must be identified. Then courses of action are specified. In this step, it is important to determine the possible consequences of each option. Sometimes leaders commit to an option and do not examine its consequences in detail. Evaluating each option and course of action is another step before comparing them because the ramifications could be quite serious.

The final step is choosing a course to pursue or creating a new course to follow. Implementing the decision and assessing the results and outcomes are necessary. While a process like this takes time, the military model is quite efficient and moves quickly, if the right team members are involved. "Adaptive leadership is an accepted leadership practice that facilitates leading in a difficult and changing environment in which we encounter adaptive and 'hybrid' threats that change and evolve tactics, techniques, and procedures across the conflict spectrum."[4]

In other decision-making models, greater emphasis is placed on objective processes. In politics, decisions are frequently made on the interests of politicians or political parties. The process involves negotiation between parties based on their interests. Some individuals personally or in professional or political venues use intuition, which is based on past experience. Solutions are determined intuitively, without applying logical or analytical reasoning. With such decisions come time pressure and other significant consequences for people, communities, and organizations.

In some circumstances, leaders must improvise because all the information is not apparent, and the world does not always work in a linear fashion. Leaders need to realize when to improvise because emotional, nonlinear, and nonquantifiable forces can derail the best laid linear plans.

An article titled "Beyond Winging It: Leadership and Improvisation," examines how following rigid plans in a dynamic, nonlinear environment is a recipe for failure.[5]

Leaders must get the job done—disequilibrium and chaos be damned! They know when to stick to a plan and when to improvise. After all, leadership is a creative force that builds imaginative relationships and interconnections that energize people to achieve and accomplish great things. How do improvisation and leadership fit together? What are the advantages and hazards of improvisation?

The world is full of hidden and interconnected fields and forces that cannot be seen or measured but that affect people and plans. The spate of leadership books dispel Newtonian notions because, if they were true, leaders would only have to implement and monitor plans and they would succeed. Books on "engineering" would dominate, not ones on the challenges and dilemmas of leadership.

Leaders face two types of decisions. Substantive decisions concern destinations—the desired goals and objectives, the "whys" and "whats" of plans. On the other hand, tactical or strategic decisions involve the processes and approaches to get to the destination—the "hows" leaders employ to achieve the "whys" and "whats." or success.

Improvisation generally affects the tactical decisions on how to reach goals and maintain integrity in an organization. Noble goals are achieved because of the great insight of leaders to read situations and respond tactically in effective and constructive ways. Many strategic decisions involve the intangibles of organizational life and the intuitive ways of knowing and understanding.

Improvisation has several key components. To institute these components requires some key characteristics. Technique is important: understanding the processes, tools, and instruments and being nimble in their application. Knowledge of the "classic" approaches and processes and having the skills to implement them are critical if a leader is to improvise. In addition, intuition, synthesis, and creativity are essential to improvising.

Paradox is a part of life, and the same is true for planning and improvisation. Just as adhering strictly to a plan can create failure, so can blind adherence to improvisation. People need to understand what drives improvisation. These drives include the following:

- **Bricolage**—Improvisation needs the skillful use and application of available resources to get the job accomplished, often with limited or different materials. Plans get stifled due to inadequate materials, either because they were lacking in the first place or there is not enough time to get them.
- **Intuition**—Time is a factor in many decisions. Frequently, judgments have to be made without hard analytical data because it is not available or cannot be obtained in time. In addition, there are forces at play that cannot be measured or seen but that affect conclusions. Leaders with a deep knowledge of their jobs understand things without formal analysis and can make choices that are necessary to achieve goals. Many know when to follow plans and when to modify or deviate from them, even when the formal data say otherwise.
- **Memory**—Leaders have knowledge and skills. They need two types of memory to improvise. First, there is declarative knowledge—facts—from which they can make sense and meaning from the patterns they see. Second, they require procedural memory—the skills and routines to get things done. Procedural skills are needed to access knowledge so that appropriate action can be taken.
- **Creativity and Learning**—Improvisation is a creative act. Conditions may call for moving beyond the script or plan. Creative leaders know how to apply procedural memory in novel ways or deviate from their normal application. There is a bit of trial and error to improvisation, which requires nimbleness and intuitive flexibility on the part of the leader.

Leadership contains some semblance of art. Management techniques and data banks and measurable indicators are available at times, but not always. But leaders cannot lead with dot-to-dot processes or tasks. It is not painting by numbers. Metrics do not tell the whole story.

The art of leadership rests on intangibles. Some musicians are highly technically proficient on their instruments but play with no emotional fervor or interpretative creativity. They play a string of notes. They don't make music. There is also interpretation and emotion in leadership.

Heart is important to accomplishment. Leaders need passion, creativity, and energy. Persistence. Finding a way to succeed. All are a part of improvising, using what you have, testing and piloting, and intuitively taking risks to adapt and adjust to the circumstances and needs of the people and situation.

The answer to leading and improvising lies in goals, values, and principles—the chords that allow improvisation with integrity. Improvisation is not everyone going their own way. It is not dissonant noise—it is harmony with values and purpose. Leaders need to act and achieve.

Great movements have "dynamic tension" between plans and circumstances—between adherence to a set strategy and adapting to the unknowns and the quirks of life. Leaders are leaders because they live for these moments and the challenges they present.

## NOTES

1. Thomas K. Varghese Jr., "How Leaders Make Decisions during Times of Crisis," Society of Thoracic Surgeons, April 24, 2020, https://www.sts.org/resources/career-resources/blog/how-leaders-make-decisions-during-times-crisis.

2. Varghese, "How Leaders Make Decisions during Times of Crisis."

3. Paula Davis, "The Art of Making Tough Decisions in a Crisis," *Forbes*, April 1, 2020.

4. Bill Cojocar, "Adaptive Leadership in the Military Decision-Making Process," *Military Review*, November–December 2011, 23–28, https://apps.dtic.mil/sti/pdfs/ADA570479.pdf.

5. George A. Goens, "Beyond Winging It: Leadership and Improvisation," GeorgeGoens.com, https://www.georgegoens.com/wp-content/uploads/2016/08/Improvising_-_Beyond_Winging_It.pdf.

*Chapter 8*

# Decisions

## *Issues and Outcomes*

There is nothing so useless as doing efficiently that which should not be done at all.

—Peter Drucker

I believe that we are solely responsible for our choices, and we have to accept the consequences of every deed, word, and thought throughout our lifetime.

—Elizabeth Kubler-Ross

Creating one's life is not easy. It is complex and not always rational or logical, and it is continually unfolding. The unexpected happens and nonrational events occur. Nature, civic actions and personal choices, and political, social, and economic modifications alter circumstances and options.

People live on a larger stage, without total control of the environment and context. Research exists on the decision-making process: how to go about making quality and successful choices. Scientific approaches suggest how to curtail or limit bias and erroneous or destructive perspectives or conclusions in research. Errors can be made that may concern the nature of the content or data.

People need the correct mindset going into a decision-making process, including issues involving leaders' perceptions of themselves and their abilities and the states of mind of others. Some of these perceptions can stifle the ability to investigate and evaluate context, issues, and processes. In a sense, participants can self-sabotage.

Self-sabotaging includes attitudes and approaches at times when people feel overwhelmed or inundated with the volume or nature of work.[1] Teamwork and problem solving take time and focus. Answers do not always come easily or clearly, particularly if the matters in question are complicated and important. Not everyone has the time to spend on difficult and possibly controversial issues that have risks for leaders who tackle them. There are other factors for individuals.

Individuals can feel overwhelmed. Despite job titles, individuals are not always self-confident. Difficult issues are not always clear and may be perceived by others as high-stakes concerns. In each situation, there are unknowns that create the possibility of highly problematic or unanticipated issues and challenges. Many leaders are highly self-critical. Success is a top priority for them because their reputation is based on it.

In taking a position, individuals are expected to address and resolve critical and difficult concerns. Some approaches can sabotage their efforts. Experience, at times, can carry some disadvantages because not all problems or issues are the same. The characters involved, the context and timing, internal and external influences, and the background and personality of leaders and others are involved. Others' past experiences or lack thereof can create different and sometimes opposing interpretations and beliefs. Relationships and motives may differ as well.

In these situations, some people default to their dominant thinking and approaches and become less flexible. Those leaders become too self-reliant and engage in micromanaging, while others may be more open-minded.

Obviously, thinking changes in difficult conditions. Different people and circumstances can freeze thought and analysis. Being cognitively and intellectually frozen or stuck stops the unconscious mind from thinking freely. Sometimes different perspectives come to mind while doing other things, such as taking a walk, driving, or relaxing.

A wandering unconscious mind is an important tool for creative problem-solving. Many leaders review the options that come to them as their mind drifts. The same is true for getting out of the context or thinking outside the box. Sometimes solutions just "pop" into one's mind.

Creative thinking goes beyond boundaries or strict rituals. There is more to it, and an individual might come up with creative answers or approaches by following a linear or process-oriented approach. Some people sleep on it and contemplate issues and subtleties. The mind works in interesting ways. Sometimes a direction or solution arises: "It just came to me!"

## RATIONAL PROCESSES

For many organizations, a rational and step-by-step process is involved to ensure objectivity and clarity among participants. Opinion is not accepted. This process includes specific steps to ensure reasonable and rational decision-making. In a Harvard Business School article, "5 Decision-Making Techniques for Managers," the author states that a process or approach is the first step to achieving results by working with and through others.[2]

Decision-making is a process, not a single event. Time is required. Framing the issue is the first step and ensures that the right questions are going to be asked. Ensuring an agreement on the question at hand is necessary so that the team can follow a multiple-step process to answer it. The team must be involved in the process to ensure multiple points of view are shared and to stimulate creativity in the problem-solving process. Participants must share knowledge with the entire group and identify any implicit biases.

This process helps develop a collaborative approach, which includes advocacy and inquiry mindsets. An advocacy mindset views decision-making as a process to persuade others and to challenge them to defend their particular positions. On the other hand, an inquiry mindset emphasizes collaborative problem-solving, where individuals test and evaluate assumptions by presenting balanced arguments, possible alternatives, and openness to constructive criticism.

Individuals in this process must feel comfortable sharing perspectives and collaborating. High-performing teams require a sense of psychological safety. Respectful discourse and active listening are essential to understanding the content and attitudes of team members.

A common pitfall is losing sight of the goals and purpose of the decision. Goals must be clear throughout the process. Revisiting the goals of the process is critical because sometimes people get lost in the details and emotions. Purpose and process must go hand in hand.

## EFFECTIVE DECISION-MAKING

Decision-making is a leader's major role. A leader must establish goals and objectives for the organization and ensure they are for the greater good of the institution. Setting direction, solving problems, addressing issues, creating a corporate culture, and managing all assets of the organization are necessary for achievement and success. To do so, leaders require conceptual understanding and emotional awareness. Some decisions are constant and others are unexpected and deeper, requiring more than simple or superficial answers.

Risk is involved beyond the routine at times. Some risks are pragmatic, and others are grounded in principle, involving greater depth and impact. A major issue for the leader is to clarify problems and determine risks and whether principles or larger concerns are involved. Leaders must check to see if the circumstances are typical or unconventional. Are there any unexplained situations or phenomena underwriting the issue? What can explain the circumstances and possible consequences?

A basic in any situation is to determine what the circumstance is really about. Sometimes managers make assumptions that are wrong about why issues erupt. A subjective judgment usually carries opinions or biases that can distort accuracy and intent. Clarity and issue identification are critically important. Sometimes people are judged incorrectly when creating or generating the issue.

Organizations confront issues all the time. The key to any resolution is determining the major problem at hand. Complex situations, complete with data, facts, impressions, interpretations, and timing, contain various propositions, pressures, unknowns, and needs. All the facts are not always readily available or certainly presented in a timely fashion.

A critical step is to clarify the issues and determine whether or not they are usual and routine or unique and exceptional. From this, defining and assessing the problem is absolutely necessary. There may be subtleties that have great influence and impact. Not everything is perceived accurately. Sometimes people do not clearly ascertain situations or issues, which deters clarity, potential responses, and effectiveness.

Specifying possible responses and answers is an obvious and evident concern. The corollary issue is what the correct response is, ethically, professionally, and humanely, in addressing circumstances. Values and norms are critical in these situations. In retrospect, the quality of a decision will be based on not only intellectual or informational insight but also principles, values, and ethics.

From here, leaders can make decisions based on necessary action: who, what, how, when, where, and why. Action also contains people's perspectives, judgments, and fears. Life is not the movies—unlike in movie scripts, reality can carry different weight and circumstances where minor energies and pressures bring about unexpected and powerful forces that affect results.

Decisions are not always easy to apply. Action sometimes gets misinterpreted or distorted. Leaders must be responsible for ensuring that any action is clearly assigned to people with the skills and knowledge to professionally carry it out. There is a larger array of decisions a leader must make:

• Who has to know of the action and who is designated to do it?

- What is necessary to ensure safety in crisis circumstances, and what time is required to ascertain the complexity of the issues? Personal or professional factors are at play in the individuals participating in the situation.

As with most decisions and situations, communication must be clear and timely. Leaders must be able to explain the philosophy, needs, and implications of decisions. Philosophy and rationale matter to a greater degree than people surmise.

## TRAPS IN DECISION-MAKING

Decisions are complex and difficult because of the context and interactions between and among those involved. Unless emergencies necessitate immediate attention and action because of safety concerns, time is necessary to ascertain the complexity of the issue. Personal or professional factors are involved with the individuals participating.

Experience, role, cognitive biases, commitments, age, and social-economic factors influence the point of view of participants. The impact of these factors depends, in part, on the nature of the decision. Personal decisions versus professional ones carry different weights and consequences. Perspectives may differ with age, training, and education. They can fill gaps in perspective or shut off cooperation and discussion.

Open discourse is necessary because closed minds or attitudes may result in insufficient or inadequate options and choices. People get trapped in their own web of thought, needs, or philosophy, limiting discourse and creativity.

At times, the escalation of emotions can inhibit relationships and connections. In these circumstances, power—formal or informal—can puncture relationships in conversation. A major detriment to problem-solving in discussion is when individuals do not feel free to talk openly and express their analyses.

In situations such as these, making quality decisions becomes hard. According to Hammond, Keeney, and Raiffa, there are hidden traps in decision-making. A major aspect is not clearly defining what decision has to be made.[3] Another is not collecting and weighing the costs and benefits of the options and ultimate decisions. Often what decision needs to be made and when are not clearly defined.

Being successful is the natural aspiration of decision-making. While action is necessary for decisions to be successful, there are some psychological traps that can get in the way.

A major issue is the anchoring trap. When presenting and discussing a situation, people frequently give disproportionate weight to the first information provided. In essence, the mind gives precedence to the first information it receives. These choices often determine when and what decisions will be made.

The status quo can also be a major trap. People are aware and work under the present circumstances; they have comfort with and a bias toward what works now. Comfort exists with the status quo even when better alternatives exist.

The third issue is the "sunk cost" trap, which is the inclination to perpetuate past mistakes and justify past choices. People stick with decision patterns they are invested in—the so-called sunk costs. It is difficult to free oneself from past decisions, even when a result is falling short or failing.

The fourth trap is only seeking supportive information and discounting any opposing data or information. People are inclined to seek out information that supports their desires or opinions by going to sites that endorse them. They decide what they want to do and then go to sources that adhere to those choices. That is not appropriate research.

In examining issues, a major concern is the framing trap. Simply put, this is misstating the problem, which undermines the entire decision-making process. The framing trap can result in finding a solution to a problem that does not exist. Framing the question at hand is necessary; if the problem is not properly defined, failure is a likely outcome. Framing affects gains and losses, so ensuring the issue is framed properly and accurately is essential.

In many organizations, leaders and teams can become overconfident because of their past success. Errors in judgment can then arise, which then leads to poor or ineffective decisions. In these situations, leaders may choose options that are familiar, discounting the uncertainty of the market or circumstances.

On the other side of the ledger, leaders can become overly prudent and fearful when making estimates about uncertain events or the future. They can take an overly cautious approach because fear of failure is a palpable force when judgment and acumen are essential.

A final issue concerns leaders' past experiences—the trap of recall ability. Like everyone else, leaders and managers experience difficult problems and challenges. When confronting new and current issues, they can give undue weight to dramatic and difficult events of the recent past; recalling these events can distort how one addresses the circumstances at hand.

To gain support and confidence, a leader must make smart, not always easy or perfect, decisions. A good decision is not always perfect. What is required is for leaders to communicate transparently how they made the choices they did, sharing data and information and the process used for defining the issue and taking the specific direction. Understanding what went into the decision gives others confidence in the process; the right people are involved, options are pursued, and people are heard. Getting feedback is important—listening is a quiet, but powerful, leadership tool.

## NOTES

1. Alice Boyes, "5 Mistakes We Make When We're Overwhelmed," *Harvard Business Review*, April 21, 2021, https://hbr.org/2021/04/5-mistakes-we-make-when-were -overwhelmed.

2. Matt Gavin, "5 Decision-Making Techniques for Managers," *Harvard Business School*, March 31, 2020, https://online.hbs.edu/blog/post/decision-making -techniques.

3. John S. Hammond, Ralph L. Keeney, and Howard Raiffa, "The Hidden Traps in Decision Making," *Harvard Business Review*, January 2006, https://hbr.org/1998/09/ the-hidden-traps-in-decision-making-2.

## Chapter 9

# Conditions and Consequences

We must never forget that we may also find meaning in life even when confronted with a hopeless situation, when facing a fate that cannot be changed. For what then matters is to bear witness to the uniquely human potential at its best, which is to transform personal tragedy into a triumph, to turn one's predicament into a human achievement.

—Viktor Frankl

Knowing oneself is not easy. It is a consistent project from childhood to adulthood, and even into old age, when one looks back in retrospect. Part of the issue is that, in a sense, individuals live in two worlds: the one they carry within themselves, and the one they confront "out there." They are not necessarily the same.

A major goal of life is "bridging between the two worlds." It raises the questions "Who am I?" and "What is this all about?"[1] People wonder about their present life and their past. They speculate how life transpired and why.

Thought is a very powerful force in life and society. John O'Donohue indicates that the identity of every person is connected to their ability to think.[2] Developing the ability to think for oneself and trusting one's instincts and perception takes courage.

Being fearful causes individuals to fall into line. The media and social or political forces present a perspective that is packaged and designed to influence. One's perspective is not the whole truth. Social media, just like individuals, have a slant, a mindset, or a frame of reference. People must truly listen for the content and intent of messages, formal, organizational, or personal.

Our society is focused on youth. Men and women use face-lifts, Botox, and clothes to forestall middle age and, God forbid, senior citizen status. Growing old comes with issues, just like childhood, adolescence, and other stages of life. At each age, some challenges are easy and others very difficult. There are family, political, and other forces painting the context of life.

79

Children's eyes, filled with innocence and wonder, see life as their family—mom, dad, brothers, and sisters. Grandparents may bring unwavering support and care. Life begins with its blank slate, and qualities are open and experiences mold consciousness, thoughts, and outlook.

Childhood is different for different people. Some experience balance and security, while others are confronted with hardships, financial difficulties, broken relationships, or violence. Some must confront the death of a parent and its impact on their lives until the end, while others sleep in the comfort of stability and consistent connection and union.

As people move into adolescence, perspectives brought by ego grow or are contained by events and their interpretation. Finding oneself socially and intellectually is a process that can be steeped in immediate recognition or through indifference. But everyone develops perspective and energy—learning and growth come from these relationships in finding the answer to the question "Who am I?"

Adulthood carries memories of growing up, family, education, and society; family still matters both in the immediacy of creating one and in providing support and stability when losses color the present and the future. Career, compensation, and responsibilities are the focus of life as adulthood takes hold. Obligation calls.

Technology is vacuous—quick and easy, but empty. Handwritten notes and letters matter and last a lifetime. Calling people and hearing their unique voice and fully understanding their personal tones and the content and intent of communication are priceless. Texts are nothing more than electronic telegrams and cannot replace a telephone call to grandparents and others while they are still here—embrace people with your presence, voice, and qualities.

So while people celebrate youth, they must not forget that with age come thinking and wisdom, the ability to relish and enjoy each moment with loved ones, and a growing understanding of why you are here and what you bring to others in the greater world. After all, life offers the opportunity to fully live the two questions everyone must answer: "Who am I?" and "Why am I here?"

## HUMAN EMOTIONS

People are amazed at artificial intelligence (AI) and what it can accomplish. They speculate on robots and what the future holds for their own success and development. At times, they speculate about artificial intelligence's memory, its cognitive analysis, and its invisible effect on daily life. Speculation exists that artificial intelligence will dominate the world and control its direction because it is more efficient than human beings.

But the fact is that human beings have multiple dimensions to them that technology can never duplicate. These aspects are what make people human beings and bring them to life. Each individual has emotions that make them human; crossing the threshold of intelligence to humanity is far beyond algorithmic machines.

Certainly, robots can perform "humanlike" behavior, such as moving about and completing tasks or navigating and sensing the environment. Humans, in fact, are much more complicated than artificial intelligence–driven machines. The human brain is very powerful and creative. Individuals are also highly social and can form relationships with others, which requires feelings and emotions—love.

Robots and low-level artificial intelligence technology operate by software programs with predictable "bot" algorithms. This bot thinking cannot produce thoughts or make judgments.[3] To improve performance, algorithms and code need to be revised. Artificial intelligence, however, can repeat the same task over and over through automation. It does not get bored.

However, cognitive bots move closer to human judgment and can improve decision-making and learning by processing larger sets of data without any human direction. Cognitive bots are not good at confronting and dealing with unexpected circumstances. They can be programmed to handle these situations through error-handling functions that direct the program to deal with it or to involve a person.

Cognitive bots require a script for these circumstances. AI does not understand context. It only operates by literally following instructions. On the other side, cognitive bots can do some things that are beyond humans. Complex calculations can be completed much quicker, and large amounts of data can be processed through searching, comparing, and moving it across systems.

The major issue with artificial intelligence technology that many people do not consider is the importance of human emotions. Technology can make decisions based on data. However, people have emotions and values that affect judgment and decisions. Life experiences teach people the importance and impact of relationships. Artificial intelligence does not have the experiences and feelings that provide and create a person's perspective and awareness. Can a computer apply ethics concretely and regularly in different situations?

Following a so-called logical algorithmic system can fall short, at times, when issues and judgments concern human interactions and reactions. Data does not quantify emotions of love, loss, fear, insight, morality, and other human qualities and traits. Sometimes things do not feel right, and individuals surpass the data and make decisions based on insight and principle.

In what questions or roles should artificial intelligence be involved? Will it make the best cognitive and emotional judgment? How much trust should individuals have in data, its nature, its collection, and its purpose and independence? Are data and its interpretation based on values and ethics?

Too many people believe that an analysis from computers, particularly if it is metrical, is the truth. Just because it comes from a computer program does not mean it is objective and free from bias. Mortimer Adler in his book *Ten Philosophical Mistakes* stated:

> Let us return to the focal point of this discussion—the distinction between knowledge and mere opinion. On the one hand, we have self-evident truths that have certitude and incorrigibility; and we also have truths that are still subject to doubt but that are supported by evidence and reasons to a degree that puts them beyond reasonable doubt or at least gives them predominance over contrary views. All else is mere opinion—with no claim to being knowledge or having any hold on truth.[4]

A major issue for adults and others is to determine what is the truth. Opinions, inferences, and fabrications are evident on the Internet and popular sites, as well as in society. Individuals must be able to discern facts from opinions and truth from speculation.

Human beings have emotional perspectives that go beyond data. Love, for example, has changed people's lives, as well as their social and professional circumstances. Love between people creates bridges and understanding. Love cannot be measured metrically and provides a standpoint artificial intelligence cannot calculate. Beauty is another ideal that is individualized, different for each person. In fact, many perspectives and emotions are unique to individuals.

Other emotions too—despair, forgiveness, gratitude, heartbreak, joy, longing, compassion, regret, shyness, and giving—provide perspective and awareness. Artificial intelligence is devoid of these attributes because it lacks heart and soul. In addition, artificial intelligence does not understand a free society and the variance in points of view inherent in it. Philosophical principles may present different options under different circumstances.

Technology can be indifferent; so can people. History holds examples of great compassion but also great indifference. Individuals' hearts and minds, however, can be awakened to the principles of humanity and hope, which are not comprehensible to the technology of daily life.

Values and ethics are at the essence of human relationships and life. They provide the core for determining what can and should be done and what is right. People are not helpless. They can act. They are not deflected from doing what is right based on principles and values.

Remember, artificial intelligence does not have a conscience or imagination. Individuals must not cede their values and ethics to machines that are unable to think at that high a level and cannot love or grieve because of their actions. After all, compassion and love are not quantitative.

## TRUTH

Frequently, people think that because something comes from a computer it must be the truth. The automation of tasks, both simple and complex, influences individuals to believe truth is built into the process and outcome.

Three types of artificial intelligence exist today.[5] ANI—artificial neural intelligence—involves machines learning and specializing in one area to solve one problem, for example, predicting the weather. The second type of artificial intelligence, AGI—artificial general intelligence—has machine intelligence, which involves "a computer that is as smart as a human across the board." AGI has human-level cognitive functions across a variety of areas: language processing, image processing, and even reasoning. The third type is ASI—artificial super intelligence. "An artificial super intelligence (ASI) system would be able to surpass all human capabilities," from decision-making and rational thinking to things like art and emotional relationships.[6]

In some cases, individuals have submitted technology or scientifically presented proposals or assessments under the guise that if it looks scientific, then it must be the truth. But studies and their validity are more complex. The quality and trustworthiness of research are based on its credibility, dependability, confirmability, and transferability. Research findings must be plausible and trustworthy; research must be able to be replicated, a clear relationship between data and findings must exist, results must be transferred to another context or group, and a continual process of engaging with the researcher is necessary.[7]

At the core of human relationships are values and ethics, as well as the emotions of despair, forgiveness, gratitude, heartbreak, joy, longing, compassion, regret, shyness, and giving. Human emotions like love and fear change people's lives and their personal and professional worlds. Love builds bridges, and beauty lies beyond an equation or statistic. To hold feelings and emotions requires values, heart, and soul, which are beyond metrical assessment.

Artificial intelligence lacks emotions like "despair, forgiveness, gratitude, heartbreak, joy, longing, compassion, regret, shyness, and giving."[8] These are all feelings that emanate from the heart, while robots' actions are defined by their algorithms or code.

Intelligence is essential to discern the truth. In some historical situations, the truth was the first victim of political priorities and debate. Emotion can cancel the truth and subvert the mind.

Dietrich Bonhoeffer discussed stupidity and truth in his book *Letters and Papers from Prison*. He stated, "Stupidity is a more dangerous enemy of the good than malice."[9] Being able to think critically is essential, as history has demonstrated in many nations; people dismiss facts, reason falls on deaf ears, prejudice restrains thought, and discussion is dismissed. Bonhoeffer also said, "But the good things like justice, truth, beauty, all great achievements, need time and steadfastness, 'memory,' or else they degenerate."[10]

Obviously, for Bonhoeffer, education is necessary for citizenry to determine the truth. Critical and objective analyses are important. Being objective requires assessing circumstances and philosophical impacts against one's personal feelings.

People must be able to discern the difference between personal and objective thinking. Sometimes individuals must go against their own feelings and the tenor of the populace and pursue a course that stands positively for truth and principles.

## PLATE SPINNERS

P. T. Barnum, in one quick phrase, stated what some advertisers and political pitchmen think: "There's a sucker born every minute." Today's political circus acts assume Barnum was right. Washington is full of jugglers, balancing acts, spinners, and tightrope walkers. In addition, equilibristics are prominent; you know, those balancing acts filled with headstands, tightrope walking, or trapeze artistry, twisting and turning from an aerial hoop and landing on their feet.

But P. T. Barnum's slogan is wrong. Suckers are made, not born. Politics is not about charismatic images, one-trick ponies that try to ride to victory, slogans without substance, or hucksters who want to sell or scare you into positions that only work to their political advantage. Supreme Court Judge Antonin Scalia stated, "Trust is won by fairly presenting the facts of the case and honestly characterizing the issues; by owning up to those points that cut against you and addressing them forthrightly; and by showing respect for the intelligence of your audience."[11]

In all professional and personal interactions, there are two kinds of communication: content and intent. Content is the topic and substance of the communication. Intent refers to the aim or purpose of the communication and its meaning and significance. Sometimes, unvarnished facts have to be identified so that the public thoroughly understands the dimension of a decision that needs to be made.

## PROFESSIONALS AND THE SOFT SIDE

Today the application of AI is promoted in many areas of life. The cognitive capabilities are fast and crisp. In health care, for example, AI analyzes patient and other data and provides a hypothesis and prescription for potential medical services. AI can enhance data analysis, diagnosis, and options for action. But is that sufficient?

Professionals do more than apply data, processes, and procedures to address complicated needs. Too often, individuals perceive professionals as technically proficient practitioners who can address our complicated needs. They expect them to be able to diagnose issues, examine data, and determine a course for improvement. It all seems so scientific and detached.

But there is more to professional practice than technical proficiency. In fact, the emotional side may be just as important. Sometimes it is the emotional side that allows individuals to trust the scientific, technical, and data-based side. Helping people includes treating not only their cognitive selves but also their emotional and soulful sides.

People are not machines or pieces of technical equipment. Just taking care of procedures or treatments is not always sufficient. Professionals also need to connect emotionally, personally, and spiritually, particularly when that interaction affects lives personally and sometimes quite dramatically.

## THINKING

Technology is supposed to help with problem-solving and decision-making. Yet individuals require solid thinking ability on their own to assess all aspects of an important issue and to make critical decisions. Thinking is not simply recalling facts and figures. It is much more. There are four important critical thinking skills—some are more complex than others.

The basic skill—convergent analytical thinking—is what most individuals perceive thinking to be: logically coming up with the best answer to the question they are facing. Memory, logic, and other resources assist in solving issues that do not require creative or lateral thinking.

A second type is divergent thinking, which is the opposite of convergent thought. It involves coming up with solutions or pathways when no single explanation exists. It involves developing several solutions to a question without a clear answer. Being able to break down possibilities into pros and cons and consider each one is an important part of the process.

Next is critical thinking. This approach requires analyzing judgments. Deductive conclusions are formulated on available facts. Induction applies critical-thinking skills to draw conclusions based on a generalization because all the facts are not available.

Creative thinking is the fourth level, which involves framing perspectives and making decisions in an unconditional or unusual manner. A creative thinker finds holes in others' thinking and proposes a different perspective, along with new or unique ways to address the issue or problem.

Different facets of life or questions require analysis, problem-solving, and creativity. Open-mindedness and flexibility are essential when examining problems and dilemmas. Posing new questions and being intellectually flexible are often needed in contending with dilemmas and new points of view.

It goes without saying that thinking is a major goal of education. Thinking is and always has been fundamental. Generally, individuals do not look at what is affecting how they think. Particularly with technology, the assumption is that it is a tool and has very little to do with people's ability to think or manner of thinking. However, even back in 1948, Harold Innis indicated that television would revolutionize American life—he was correct.[12] Americans spend on average roughly half of their waking hours in front of a screen. Entertainment is not academics, and television does not encourage reading or thinking.

Today, technology has grown enormously, and now society uses artificial intelligence, which has an impact on life and education. One concern about the education of today's students is the erosion of deep literacy, according to Adam Garfinkel.[13] The premise is that the brain "wires itself continuously in accordance with its every experience." Today children and others spend a great amount of time in front of a technology screen, which affects new and existing cognitive capacities.

> Deep literacy is what happens when a reader engages with an extended piece of writing in such a way as to anticipate an author's direction and meaning, and engages what one already knows in a dialectical process with the text. The result . . . is a fusion of writer and reader, with the potential to bear original insight.[14]

Deep literacy involves abstract thought and entails raising difficult questions. Creativity and imagination are spurred, along with personal, social, and cultural insight. Reading novels, history, and other genres has emotional aspects as well, raising empathy, anxiety, amusement, fear, pride, love, and other feelings. Greater understanding is the result.

Deep reading requires an attention span in order to comprehend the literature and apply abstract reasoning. Digital devices are designed to be addictive, and they "discretely hijack our attention. To the extent that you cannot perceive the world around you in its fullness, to the same extent you will fall back into mindless, repetitive, self-reinforcing behavior, unable to escape."[15] In a sense, individuals cannot slow down enough to focus quality attention on a complex problem. Without that, individuals cannot think effectively or thoroughly.

Some young people seem preoccupied and give only partial attention to a task at hand. Multitasking causes individuals to lose focus. When machines are programmed by others to make decisions for the individual, ethics and morality can be violated because the individual is not confronting the issues and alternatives and making decisions—the algorithmic computer is.

Reading books is extremely important for being well educated and understanding complicated situations and the truth. Henry Kissinger, former secretary of state, stated in his book *World Order*:

> But philosophers and poets have long separated the mind's purview into three components: information, knowledge, and wisdom. The Internet focuses on the realm of information, whose spread it facilitates exponentially. Search engines are able to handle increasingly complex questions with increasing speed. Yet a surfeit of information may paradoxically inhibit the acquisition of knowledge and push wisdom even further away than it was before.
>
> The poet T. S. Eliot captured this in his "Choruses from 'The Rock'": "Where is the Life we have lost in living? Where is the wisdom we have lost in knowledge? Where is the knowledge we have lost in information?"[16]

Technology today makes information extremely accessible; however, this brings with it new issues. Just because the avalanche of information on the Web is available does not make it significant. Determining what is and what is not significant is a major issue because individuals can communicate instantaneously. The old adage "Don't believe everything you read [or hear]" is extremely pertinent in today's society.

Learning from books is much more personal than on the Web. Details and philosophy are provided, and individuals have to engage in conceptual thinking, which involves recognizing and understanding data, events, and concepts. Books are deep on substance and in details about the author's position and its development.

The former governor of Wisconsin wanted to remove the words "search for truth" from the mission statement of the University of Wisconsin and replace it with a lame statement: "meet the state's workforce needs."[17] For some politicians, truth is dangerous. But the country needs citizens who search for truth. Democracy needs skeptics, not sheep.

Skepticism is not negative. It is essential for determining the truthfulness of politicians, the media, or other sources. The ability to comprehend, analyze, and evaluate ideas, propositions, and proposals is necessary in private life, as well as socially and civically. Being skeptical requires cognitive skills and is fundamental to being a critical thinker and an active citizen in a democratic republic. Educated people ask questions and try to discern the truth; they see through distortions, self-interest, and unethical use of data, research, and information.

Skepticism applies reason to complex thinking in order to determine whether arguments, assumptions, or proposals are valid. It is absolutely essential in order to expose "junk" thought and other forms of deception. In this political age, cynicism is not needed, but skepticism is.

The term *skeptic* is derived from the Greek *skeptikos*, meaning "to inquire" or "to question." Skeptics examine information, analyze it, and require more information and data to determine whether proposals or positions are true or realistic. They do not just accept recommendations or proposals because they are presented authoritatively.

Critical thinkers challenge sources, interpretations, and conclusions of data and information. Accepting opinions or statements purely on the basis of beliefs is dangerous. Politicians, media, and organizations should have to substantiate their judgments or claims on facts and knowledge, not simply give opinions or dogma.

A basic question is this: What is the truth? How does one know what is opinion and propaganda and what is in the sphere of truth? Howard Gardner, in his book *Truth, Beauty, and Goodness Reframed*, asks, "How best can we establish the status of truth in a postmodern, digital era? By showing the power but also the limitations of sensory knowledge. By explaining the methods whereby the several disciplines—mathematics, science, history—go about arriving at their accounts of the world and arriving at their respective truths. By demonstrating how we evaluate disciplinary evidence—and the evidence from multiple disciplines—in determining truth value."[18]

Gardner states that young people prefer to get their "news" on social media, particularly from sources with which they agree. In a sense, some individuals reside in valleys of opinion that simply echo their points of view. The Internet has no editorial filters or checks for accuracy or impartiality. Anyone can post opinions, speculation, or propaganda.

The search for truth is and should continue to be the purpose of education today. "Fake knowledge," "false news," and "junk science" permeate discussions in today's media. All of these are examples of instability because of their disrespect for the standards of truth, communication, and democracy. As a result, people become exasperated and lose faith in the integrity of news agencies and other institutions.

Philosophically, the answer to the question "What is truth?" would seem easy. Either something is true and can be proved, or it is false and does not exist. Philosopher Mortimer Adler stated, "When a person speaks truthfully it follows necessarily that what he thinks is true in fact."[19]

## SKEPTICISM: TRUTH AND EDUCATION

Education is about pursuing the truth. Truth and honesty obviously have connections. All educated people should question, reflect, and study to find objective truth and reality in science, governance, and other areas. In some cases, discoveries may supplant what was previously thought and accepted.

In matters of truth, dispute and dialogue are fruitful. When examining the veracity of opinions, proposals, and judgments, civil conversations with those who disagree can be enlightening. A civil debate can uncover assumptions, facts, or philosophical dispositions that threaten or divert the search for truth. Too frequently today, people abandon discussion in a fit of incivility, thereby deserting the pursuit of truth. Comedian George Carlin got it right: "Don't just teach your children to read . . . teach them to question everything that they read . . . teach them to question everything."[20]

Credibility rests on truthfulness. Our politics and the deceitful campaigns of both Democrats and Republicans are destroying the fabric of honesty and credibility needed to unite a country and lead based on the values of truth in thought, speech, and action.

The congruence between words and deeds is essential in a democracy. If its citizens cannot trust the government or its leaders to be truthful, then our country is threatened from within by cynicism, apathy, and separation. Vietnam, Watergate, and Gitmo are all examples of deception and broken promises.

Truth is an absolute. It is not a relative value, and deceptiveness reduces moral standards. Candidates use political gunslingers like David Axelrod and Karl Rove to obfuscate and deceive in order to push the body politic toward a rush to judgment or groupthink. The means and ends of political discourse should be truthful and carry moral reasoning, not expedients to push a poll number that in itself may come from questionable data.

Character assassination, distortions, half truths, frivolous diversions, and lies drag the political process precariously close to divorce from any credible thought. Any semblance of integrity in the system is curtailed as mature discussion of issues is avoided in the interest of expedience.

What both candidates demonstrate is a lack of moral courage. Telling the truth may not be popular, but it is the right thing to do. Leaders with moral courage do not tell people what they want to hear but what they need to know. It would be quite refreshing for citizens to hear candidates candidly describe and explain the issues of the day and their plans to address them.

But platitudes win, and truthfulness is shelved for self-interest at the expense of the common good.

Moral courage is doing what is right and accepting the consequences. The sad state of our politics belies any semblance of moral courage in both parties. Candidates become attached to power and their own electoral self-interest.

People scoff at candidates and say, "Why listen to the them? They all lie anyway." Leaders who are party to deceptive, untruthful, or dishonest campaigns lose trust and lower the moral standard for the country. They set a poor example for youth and others by their deception, and they weaken the democracy they all say they want to see prosper.

Finally, leaders who are not trusted will not be able to challenge others to greatness. Truthfulness matters, particularly when there are hard truths that citizens have to consider. Elective office is not about the future of the incumbents or those who aspire to power. Serving the public is really about honesty with the citizens and the democracy they cherish. And the hard truth matters.

## NOTES

1. John O'Donohue and John Quinn, *Working in Wonder: Eternal Wisdom for a Modern World* (New York: Crown, 2018), 5.

2. O'Donohue and Quinn, *Working in Wonder*, 32.

3. WorkFusion, "How a Bot Thinks: Differences between Robots and Humans," August 23, 2019, https://www.workfusion.com/blog/how-a-bot-thinks-differences-between-robots-and-humans/.

4. Mortimer J. Adler, *Ten Philosophical Mistakes* (New York: Touchstone, 1985), 100–101.

5. Vaishali Advani, "What Is Artificial Intelligence? How Does AI Work, Types and Future of It?," *Great Learning* (blog), October 19, 2021, https://www.pye.ai/2021/02/11/what-is-artificial-intelligence-how-does-ai-work-types-and-the-future-of-it/.

6. Advani, "What Is Artificial Intelligence?"

7. Advani, "What Is Artificial Intelligence?"

8. WorkFusion, "How a Bot Thinks."

9. Dietrich Bonhoeffer, *Letters and Papers from Prison* (Minneapolis: Fortress, 2015), 9.

10. Bonhoeffer, *Letters and Papers from Prison*, 278.

11. Stephen Liebb, "How to Persuade a Judge," *San Quentin News*, November 1, 2008, https://sanquentinnews.com/how-to-persuade-a-judge/.

12. Harold Innis, *The Bias of Communication* (Toronto: University of Toronto, 1951), 28.

13. Adam Garfinkel, "The Erosion of Deep Literacy," *National Affairs* (Spring 2020), https://nationalaffairs.com/publications/detail/the-erosion-of-deep-literacy.

14. Garfinkel, "The Erosion of Deep Literacy."

15. Garfinkel, "The Erosion of Deep Literacy."

16. Henry Kissinger, *World Order* (New York: Penguin, 2014), 349.

17. Patrick Marley and Jason Stern, "Records: Scott Walker Wanted Wisconsin Idea Changes," *Milwaikee Journal Sentinel*, May 27, 2016, https://archive.jsonline.com/news/statepolitics/judge-orders-scott-walker-to-release-emails-on-wisconsin-idea-b99733921z1-381151041.html/.

18. Howard Gardner, *Truth, Beauty, and Goodness Reframed* (New York: Basic Books, 2011), 45–46.

19. Mortimer Adler, *How to Think about the Great Ideas*, rev. ed. (Chicago: Open Court, 2000), 3.

20. George Carlin, "Question Everything," YouTube, VinmanaRama, June 24, 2008.

*Chapter 10*

# The Path of Life

He who has a why to live for can bear almost any how.

—Friedrich Nietzsche

When people think about their life or the lives of their children and loved ones, the focus is on happiness and success. Parents want their children to be content, live a good life, and find fulfillment.

Unfortunately, some individuals do not persevere and address their needs; they stop learning and adjusting to circumstances. Instead of continuing to learn and grow, they become barnacles. "The barnacle is confronted with an existential decision about where it's going to live. Once it decides . . . it spends the rest of its life with its head cemented to a rock."[1]

American society historically and metaphorically is premised on autonomy, self-sufficiency, and independence for its citizens. The prototype American is a can-do, independent individual with the liberty and latitude to care for themselves. Freeloading and panhandling are the opposite of the "American way" and its values. Individuals are supposed to be independent and self-sufficient people.

Real life is not the movies. How life unfolds is far different than scripts defining who is a character, what they want and need, and why they cannot have it, all in a ninety-minute movie.

Fictional diversions are entertaining, but life itself is much more intense and difficult. One thing all children should know is that they need to learn from failures and successes. There is something to be learned in both circumstances. Learning occurs through experience and life, struggling and suffering, and dealing with things that individuals cannot change. The ability to keep on working and confronting life positively and through their capabilities is essential.

Life is not always an easy trip, which in every case has an ending. Life requires understanding and commitment, strong values and principles, endurance and emotional strength, and confronting successes and failures. Understanding what is significant and what is superficial is very important. Being true to oneself is a personal path, not one formed by others. A meaningful life is not created by winning a prize or obtaining fame. It is deeper than that and engages all aspects of one's being, physically, emotionally, intellectually, and philosophically.

## MEANING

Happiness is one thing in life that can flow from enjoyable experiences, pleasure, or achieving difficult goals. A scientist might say it comes from an increase in serotonin because higher levels of this chemical increase feelings of confidence, well-being, and belonging. Either way, it comes from within— life decisions and choosing to be positive and happy. Happiness rests in one's heart and in assisting others to find happiness. Knowing oneself and being sincere and "real" are critical in pleasure and contentment.

Meaning cannot be purchased; it is built from past experiences, beliefs, virtues, and one's relationships and love, including the values one is willing to sacrifice for. In a sense, living one's positive values is a means to pursue and find a satisfying and happy life.

Doing the right thing includes treating others justly, with fairness and decency. Justice and virtue through positive ethic leads one to interact with others and make decisions in a moral and fair-minded manner. Respectful and upright treatment of others is necessary in developing honorable and proper relationships. Virtue ethics—doing the right thing and treating people fairly and decently—are stepping-stones to a decent and constructive life.[2]

All individuals must live a life in which they are sincere and true to themselves. Living to please others is not a road to fulfillment or happiness because it is based on the expectations and desires of others.

Life unfolds continually because everyone learns things about themselves, emanating from experiences, successes, and failures. In a sense, everyone has an internal dialogue with themselves.

In that regard, meaning unfolds through self-understanding, relationships, experiences, philosophy, and principles and beliefs.

> Meaning is not something you stumble across, like the answer to a riddle or
> the prize in a treasure hunt. Meaning is something you build into your life. You
> build it out of your own past, out of your affections and loyalties, out of the
> experience of humankind as it is passed on to you, out of your own talent and

understanding, out of the things you believe in, out of the things and people you love, out of the values for which you are willing to sacrifice something. The ingredients are there. You are the only one who can put them together into that unique pattern that will be your life. Let it be a life that has dignity and meaning for you. If it does, then the particular balance of success or failure—as the world measures success or failure—is of less account.[3]

Many people think that life is not a continuous path of self-discovery. Some speculate one's early years are the ones in which learning takes place and where wisdom is developed. But, when older people talk of life, they frequently state that wisdom unfolds through self-discovery and the endless and often unpredictable situations in which they find themselves. Discovery and the endless circumstances of life create a continual dialogue between the self and the situations and relationships that unfold. The world, as many people know, continues to impact society, nature, and one's own potentialities and responses.

In each phase of life, individuals seek meaning. Everyone wonders and seeks experiences that will affect their growth and opportunities. People pursue meaning to understand themselves. Everyone, at some point, realizes that life ends, and finding a positive path to meaning nourishes the body and soul to continue the journey.

Meaning involves personal identity and is nurtured from a variety of sources. Some are emotional, some intellectual, and some come from social or intellectual beliefs or roots. Meaning "implies a relationship between the person and some larger system of ideas or values, a relationship involving obligations as well as rewards."[4]

Values provide a framework to determine and analyze the impact of events and circumstances and the meaning of them on one's life. Every event and piece of information is evaluated for its impact on individuals and their direction of life. At times, this impact can assist individuals or disrupt their lives.

Life does not always unfold like a systematic flowchart. Disruptions occur. The lives of others speed up or slow progress; changing times result in changing expectations. Distinctive data or information challenges or conflicts with goals and intentions and may distract individuals intellectually and physically.

Optimism emanates from the possibility to achieve important goals. Achieving personal goals is a means to happiness. Not all people have the same desires or ambitions; life unfolds differently for every individual. Examining the life of various individuals demonstrates that there are alternative pathways to a happy life. Each person, however, must understand and select personal aims in order to find satisfaction and happiness.

According to Martin Seligman,[5] reaching goals in life requires several things: obviously, wisdom based on virtues, which involves curiosity, learning, judgment, and creativity. A second cluster concerns courage, valor, perseverance, and integrity. A third concerns humanity and love, which involves intimacy, kindness, sociability, and intelligence. In addition, justice, concerning citizenship, fairness, and leadership, is required. Temperance and the strengths of forgiveness, humility, and self-regulation are necessary, along with transcendence and appreciation for beauty, gratitude, hope, humor, and spirituality.[6]

In essence, meaning is connected to something larger than self. A life of meaning exceeds pleasantry and engagement. Life requires understanding one's strengths and applying them to serious issues larger than oneself. Being in the "flow" emanates from this perspective.

According to psychologists, there's a sequence of steps to individuals developing "who they are" and "what they want to achieve in life."[7] In sequence, the steps include the following:

> Each man or woman starts with a need to preserve the self, to keep the body and its basic goals from disintegrating. At this point the meaning of life is simple; it is tantamount to survival, comfort, and pleasure. When the safety of the physical self is no longer in doubt, the person may expand the horizon of his or her meaning system to embrace the values of a community—the family, the neighborhood, a religious or ethnic group. This step leads to a greater complexity of the self, even though it usually implies conformity to conventional norms and standards.
>
> The next step in development involves reflective individualism. The person again turns inward, finding new grounds for authority and value within the self. He or she is no longer blindly conforming, but develops an autonomous conscience. At this point the main goal in life becomes the desire for growth, improvement, the actualization of potential.
>
> The fourth step, which builds on all the previous ones, is a final turning away from the self, back toward an integration with other people and with universal values. In this final stage the extremely individualized person—like Siddhartha letting the river take control of his boat—willingly merges his interests with those of a larger whole.[8]

## ADVERSITY

Parents and families want their children and relatives to have success and a good life filled with achievement and contentment. A major aspect is for them to reach their goals and dreams. The problem with this is that life happens: success, failure, uncertainty, doubt, achievement, recognition, surprise, and more come.

Life, however, does not always work out as dreamed or anticipated. There are external issues that get in the way—health and death, social and economic issues, foresight and experiences, and other issues and events. Both success and failure are important in life because there is something to be learned from each.

In life, lessons are continual. When one gets older, these learning experiences and issues become clearer. And in some cases, one can see that past behavior and decisions were inappropriate, shallow, vacant, or even embarrassing. The issue is to learn from these and other experiences. These times between success or failure can be valuable and beneficial to examine issues and find alternative directions or answers.

Experiences raise the question of what people can learn from them. Lessons are not always easy. Suffering is a part of life. Some of the toughest issues concern things individuals cannot control or change. Gardner states:

> The things you learn in maturity aren't simple things such as acquiring information and skills. You learn not to engage in self-destructive behavior. You learn not to burn up energy in anxiety. You discover how to manage your tensions, if you have any, which you do. You learn that self-pity and resentment are among the most toxic of drugs. You find that the world loves talent, but pays off on character.[9]

In all of this, individuals apply knowledge, values, intelligence, and philosophical perspective. In doing so, they discover who they are. They see themselves and realize what their philosophical dispositions are, and they can come to terms with who they are, their values and priorities.

Things are not always clear. We often wonder why events happened as they did. In such disconcerting times, people examine their faults and move to be better through resilience and stamina.[10] Americans have to overcome self-indulgence and be and do better.

In reflecting about situations and circumstances, people have regrets. Many regrets are based on not having the courage to be true to themselves but instead acting on the expectations or desires of others. Individuals have to be true to themselves. Philosophy, skills, and experiences provide perspective about life and one's role and contribution to oneself, others, and society.

Aristotle believed that people should be trained in logic and in questioning premises. These are critical skills for defining and expressing oneself. Questioning is important; obtaining clarity on issues and proposals is essential in personal, social, or professional relationships.[11]

## SELF

Everyone has to build themselves a life. As children, people use their imagination to think and dream about what their lives are going to be like in the
future. Of course, many scenarios involve happiness, goodness, heroism, and
other desires and fantasies.

In these times, people strive for success as a means to satisfaction and happiness. However, age works its influence on life's ventures and perspective,
some people sense a loss of competence and physical capabilities and, in
some cases, philosophical acceptance and tolerance.

As time passes, individuals judge their self-worth based on their job performance and whether it is positive or negative. Some perceive themselves
through the lens of their job. They believe, "I am my job." As people have
discovered over various economic times, jobs may change, but people cannot
abandon themselves.

The drive for success often stymies one's personal life. Some people do not
realize that when retirement ensues, they must once again face the question
"Who am I?" Their old job title no longer describes them or their life. They
forget that there is a unique human being behind each job title.

Arthur C. Brooks expresses concern for people who "objectify" themselves. He asks:

- Is your job the biggest part of your identity? Is it the way you introduce
  yourself or even understand yourself?
- Do you find yourself sacrificing love relationships for work? Have you
  forgone romance, friendship, or starting a family because of your career?
- Do you have trouble imagining being happy if you were to lose your
  job or career? Does the idea of losing it feel a little like death to you?[12]

People who respond positively to any or all of these questions basically
objectify themselves as their profession. A career should be an extension of
oneself, not vice versa. A good life is not your job or profession. It is about
who you are as a human being.

People need to get away from work. Individuals must spend time with
the people they love. People who love their work or profession should get
time away via vacations or other means. Doing so gives individuals time for
diversion and reflection, which will provide creativity. Time in silence away
from work allows insights to develop and perspectives to sharpen. Creativity
requires silence and time away from the daily grind.

## CHALLENGES

Life has challenges, no matter one's education or family resources or any other aspect of life. Some people must confront highly difficult emotional and physical issues and professional challenges. Some navigate these situations; others do not.

How people deal with challenges is affected by how they interpret them. Some see challenges as something to overcome, while others perceive them as threats. Csikszentmihalyi identified people who translate threats into challenges, the result of which is "inner harmony."[13] He explains that people who perceive threats as challenges have an "autotelic" self—a person who is seldom bored or anxious, has self-contained goals, and is highly involved with what is happening. These individuals:

- Set clear goals
- Learn to make choices in life, from long commitments to trivial decisions
- Recognize challenges and commit to them and are sensitive to input
- Consistently pay attention to what is happening and concentrate
- Learn to enjoy the experience, even when things do not go well

Life is not always a smooth ride, but everyone has a choice in how they respond. Some individuals confront tough times and life events. Others less so. The death of a parent is a very difficult and dramatic event that steers individuals off course because they feel they do not have choices. "But if one assumes that people have a choice in how they respond to external events, and what meaning they attribute to suffering, then one can interpret the constructive response as normal and the neurotic one as a failure to rise to the challenge."[14]

## MEANING

People learn throughout their lives. Looking back, they realize what life is and what it offers. But the actual definition of a meaningful life is not easy to discover. For some, it involves relationships, family, and happiness, which are connected to love and financial security. For others, philosophically, a good life is related to one of health, wellness, and longevity.

According to one study, "when you find more meaning in life, you become more contented, whereas if you don't have purpose in life and are searching for it unsuccessfully, you'll feel more stressed out."[15]

Meaning in life changes with age. In the thirties to sixties, relationships are more established, as well as family life and career. Life changes later with age sixty-five and after—retirement. Titles and positions change. Relatives and friends pass away. Health issues may begin to arise. People in this age category start searching for meaning—what has life been about?

Finding more meaning is essential for well-being and health. Commitments in life, ethical standards, family, and human connections are important. Isolation, lack of purpose, and loss are powerful and damaging factors in curtailing meaning.

All people seek meaning: where they fit into the scheme of things. A sense of meaninglessness is a difficult and disruptive force and mentality. Finding meaning does not happen on a schedule. For some, meaning comes early and for others later. Meaning can be very emotional and for some very intellectual. But the different kinds of meaning all involve relationships between the individual and a larger system of ideals or values, which involves obligations and commitments.[16]

Finding meaning sometimes involves suffering. Difficult things happen in life. Sometimes suffering provides the incentive to nurture an individual's interests and skills. The assumption is that they have a choice in how they respond. As a victim? Or as an actor, someone who can pursue positive outcomes? Seeing oneself as victimized is a pathway to subordinating to events. Great things occur because people produce harmony and achievement over chaos.

Viktor Frankl indicated that meaning in life is what people choose to give it. He showed that those who survived the concentration camps did so not because of physical strength but through retaining a sense of control over their attitudes. He said:

> We who lived in concentration camps can remember the men who walked through the huts comforting others, giving away their last piece of bread. They may have been few in number, but they offer sufficient proof that everything can be taken from a man but one thing: the last of human freedoms—to choose one's own attitude in any given set of circumstances—to choose one's own way.[17]

In this statement, a sense of control, even a minor sense, is important. Even in dire times, control can be found through changing one's attitude. Creativity in these dire times is giving something back to the world through self-expression. Another major issue is the experience of interacting authentically with others and the context. Authenticity confirms honesty and dependability.

Freedom is necessary for a good life, where individuals have a semblance of responsibility based on values and management of their own decisions and choices. Freedom comes from understanding rights and resources, as well as the ability to self-regulate and make proper choices. A life of meaning is far removed from just seeking pleasure in one's own life, but it is found in serving others and in one's values and beliefs. This is a larger contribution than simply pursuing pleasures.

## WISDOM

Wisdom is a virtue that is important to personal and public life and endeavors. It is far removed from profits, fame, and self-interest. It concerns meeting human needs and also justice, equality, and human rights, which have been staples in life and relationships over centuries. It comes from applying curiosity, a love of learning, and a commitment to justice. People have responsibility for their decisions.

Everyone wants a life free from suppression and fiscal and physical needs. To find this, individuals have to contribute and respect the efforts of others. Freedom carries with it the responsibility to examine one's own life and behavior, as well as what is transpiring locally and nationally.

All individuals want to find a purpose in life that unifies and justifies what they do. Purpose attracts and mobilizes individuals to goals, ambitions, and objectives. Challenges need to be faced in order to address life's conditions and purpose. In these processes and endeavors, individuals develop and comprehend who they are, what they need in life, and why they are here.

## NOTES

1. John W. Gardner, *Living, Leading, and the American Dream*, Kindle edition (Jossey-Bass, 2003), loc. 593.

3. Edith Hall, *Aristotle's Way: How Ancient Wisdom Can Change Your Life* (New York: Penguin, 2019), 30.

3. Gardner, *Living, Leading, and the American Dream*, loc. 746.

4. Gardner, *Living, Leading, and the American Dream*, loc. 1007.

5. Martin E. P. Seligman, Positive Psychology Center, ppc.sas.upenn.edu.

6. Martin E. P. Seligman, "Afterword: Breaking the 65 Percent," in *A Life Worth Living: Contributions to Positive Psychology*, eds. Mihaly Csikszentmihalyi and Isabella Selega Csikszentmihalyi (Oxford: Oxford University Press, 2006), 233.

8. Mihaly Csikszentmihalyi, *Flow: The Psychology of Optimal Experience* (New York: HarperCollins, 2008), 221.

9. Csikszentmihalyi, *Flow*, 221.

8. Gardner, *Living, Leading, and the American Dream*, loc. 631.

10. Gardner, *Living, Leading, and the American Dream*, loc. 2296.

11. Hall, *Aristotle's Way*, 78, 80–84.

12. Arthur C. Brooks, "A Profession Is Not a Personality," *Atlantic*, September 30, 2021, https://www.theatlantic.com/family/archive/2021/09/self-objectification-work /620246/.

14. Csikszentmihalyi, *Flow*, 209.

13. Csikszentmihalyi, *Flow*, 234.

15. Pranjal Mehar, "What Is the Real Meaning of Life? A Study Found the Answer," *Tech Explorist*, December 11, 2019, https://www.techexplorist.com/what -real-meaning-life-study-found-answer/28461/.

17. Gardner, *Living, Leading, and the American Dream*, loc. 1007.

16. Quoted in Neel Burton, "What Is the Meaning of Life?" *Psychology Today* (January 2021).

www.ingramcontent.com/pod-product-compliance
Lightning Source LLC
Chambersburg PA
CBHW020358270326
41926CB00007B/485